'It is my favourite of Bryony's books.' Dolly Alderton

'This is a book that tears down walls. It will make sobriety attractive and accessible in a way it never has before.' Marian Keyes

'This book will make us all kinder, brighter and better.' Daisy Buchanan

'Bryony Gordon is a terrific, compassionate writer whose razor-sharp honesty slices through every sentence of this compelling memoir.' Elizabeth Day

'Poetic, raw and very important.' Fearne Cotton

'Bryony Gordon has penned a compelling, candid sobriety memoir.' *Independent*

'An unflinching memoir ... harrowing but ultimately hopeful, this is essential reading.' *Red*

'This very readable book is a crucial reminder that change – of any kind – isn't going to happen with a quick fix but that sometimes it can truly hurt and undo us but that there _____ places.' *Stylist*

In the twenty years that she has worked for the *Telegraph*, Bryony Gordon has become one of the paper's best-loved writers. She is the author of the *bestselling The Wrong Knickers* plus *The Sunday Times* Number One bestsellers *You Got This* and *Mad Girl*, which were both nominated for British Book Awards. She is the presenter of the Mad World podcast and in 2016 she founded Mental Health Mates, now a peer support network that encourages people with mental health issues to connect and get out of the house. In 2017 she won the MIND Making A Difference Award for her work in changing the perception of mental health in the media. She lives in South London with her husband and daughter, and their two guinea pigs.

Also by Bryony Gordon:
The Wrong Knickers: A Decade of Chaos
Mad Girl
Eat, Drink, Run
You Got This
No Such Thing As Normal

BRYONY GORDON

GLORIOUS ROCK BOTTOM

HEADLINE

For Holly

First published in the UK in 2020 by
HEADLINE PUBLISHING GROUP

First published in paperback in 2021 by
HEADLINE PUBLISHING GROUP

1

Cataloguing in Publication Data is available from the British Library

ISBN 978 1 4722 5377 4

Typeset in Berling by Palimpsest Book Production Ltd, Falkirk, Stirlingshire

Printed and bound in Great Britain by Clays Ltd, Elcograf S.p.A.
Designed by Siobhan Hooper

Headline's policy is to use papers that are natural, renewable and recyclable
products and made from wood grown in well-managed forests and other
controlled sources. The logging and manufacturing processes are expected to
conform to the environmental regulations of the country of origin.

HEADLINE PUBLISHING GROUP
An Hachette UK Company
Carmelite House
50 Victoria Embankment
London
EC4Y 0DZ

www.headline.co.uk
www.hachette.co.uk

Contents

Preface

The book you are holding in your hand might not always be easy to read. It certainly wasn't always easy to write – in fact, I did almost everything I could not to sit down and start it. In the end, it burnt its way out of my body. I was as powerless over the words falling onto the page as I had been over the alcohol that had held me in its grip. Putting my experiences down on paper was often painful and often shocking, even to me, but it had to be done.

Even in the editing process, I had to force myself to go back over what I'd written. I would reluctantly be going through a chapter and find my breath catching in my chest at the awfulness of my behaviour. Was that really me?

1

Yes. Yes, it was.

And maybe it is you, too. Or perhaps it is someone you know and love. The truth is, alcoholism affects every section of society, but we find it easier to pretend otherwise: we shrug it off as a bit of a laugh, this thing that can slowly destroy the soul. Alcohol is legal. It's sold in supermarkets. How bad can it be? We tell ourselves that alcoholics sit on park benches, with insurmountable problems, that they have lost everything and been driven to drink. And sometimes they are this person: but they are many other types of people, too. I see this in the messages I receive on Instagram and in my inbox, from so-called 'normal' people just like me or you, asking for advice on how to give up drinking. I wish I could give these people some magic cure-all. But all I can really tell them is that the shame attached to alcoholism is what kept me in it for so long, and once I began to let that go I could start to find peace.

That's why I wanted to write this difficult book, with all its awful unvarnished truths. Because the truth hurts, but it also heals. It is the only way out of the nightmare of addiction. And oh, the absolute joys that wait for you on the other side! Acceptance, friendship, love and hope – they are in this book too, so it's not *all* bad.

I want to be clear, right from the outset, that this book contains only my truth. I don't pretend to be an expert on alcoholism, only someone who has experienced it, and I have changed the names and details of many people who feature in this book because it is not my place to force them into revealing their truths, too. At the end of the book you will find a list of resources that you can turn to should you feel you need help. Do not be ashamed to reach out for that help as soon as you can. For there is no shame in living in your truth.

1

Never again

There was a conker on the ground.

A fucking conker.

Hard, shiny, obscene, it glared its polished arse at me as if it had every right to be there. As if *I* was the one who had arrived early and unwelcome, the one who was in the wrong. What was it doing there, this grotesque, swollen, overgrown seed that signalled the end of all that was good: summer holidays, tanned shoulders, endless glasses of rosé in pub gardens.

It was August. It was fucking *August*. This conker was a month premature. It had fallen too soon. The ground wasn't ready for it. More importantly, I wasn't ready for it. I had plans for this summer. More plans. Seemingly endless plans that involved drinking, for these were the only plans I could make that would consistently come to fruition. Plans that involved *not* drinking rarely made it past the early light of day, when I would make vague promises to myself to get them done tomorrow. Or the day after tomorrow. Or Monday. Or next month, next year, next life, and so on and so on until I choked on my own vomit or fell down a flight of stairs or was thrown out of the house by my husband, who despite being married to a lunatic was not an actual lunatic himself.

And that was the problem with the conker, the problem with life, the problem with *everything*, really. This moment signalled the end of things: things that had to change by the time autumn arrived and my four-year-old daughter started school. That was, we had agreed – I had agreed – going to be the end of it all. All of this. All of that. The slurring, the scuffing, the disappearing, the drinking. It would be done. Really done. In a week's time we would draw a line under it, a line I would not be tempted to snort, and then we would move on. We would forget all about it, except when we laughed about it. Hahahahahahaha, wasn't my drunken behaviour hilarious? But the look on my husband's face would tell me that it had never been funny, not even back before parenthood and adulthood and everythinghood. This was not a joke, or a punchline to one. This was very, very serious.

At what level, in my body, did I know that the party was over? That the party had been over for some time, that it had never actually been that good a party anyway? That warm summer's evening, as I stared at the conker, I knew what was coming. I knew it in my cells, which had been quivering and collapsing in on themselves for some time. I knew it in my skin, the skin I wanted to scratch off so I could start again. The end was nigh. I was a blighted chestnut tree, waiting to be put out of my misery, and I was going to have to destroy myself to have any hope of rising again.

So.

Well.

That is what I set out to do.

It was early Friday night, the Friday of the August bank holiday. I had told Harry that I was only going out for a couple of drinks, even though I had never managed to have a couple of drinks ever in my life. Maybe once, but only because I was feeling hungover and ill from the night before. Harry looked at me with resigned fury. In the living room, our daughter played happy families with some small furry toy animals. I loved my family deeply, but all the love in the world could not quieten or still the chaos in my head quite as effectively as I believed alcohol could. My husband reminded me that we needed to leave the house early the next day to drive to his dad's for the weekend. He said that I should 'bear that in mind', as if I was a human who needed careful instruction, a teenage child perhaps. 'Of course!' I beamed, kissing him on the cheek. 'I can't wait for a weekend away.'

I walked out the door with the bounce of a woman who had once again got away with it, and couldn't quite believe it. Harry did not try to stop me. He had no choice but to be complicit. Was it worse for him, in some strange way? I was out of control but I at least had my hand on the brake, even if I never actually applied it. He was just a passenger. There was nothing he could do but trust that I would somehow turn things round, instead of crashing us all into the central reservation.

I picked up the conker from the pavement, took a picture of it and posted it on Instagram. I captioned it simply: winter is coming. It was almost over. It was almost done. I was going to have to go out and drink all the alcohol in London, all the alcohol in the world, before I had my privileges taken away from me. I could not think of anything other than my desperate need to get to the pub and secure a seat outside so I could chain-smoke and neck pints of ale. Ale was the thing, I had discovered. It tasted like sour fruit but I had long ago resigned myself to the fact that I didn't drink booze for the taste. It had slightly less alcohol than lager, which meant I could drink it for longer. And choosing to drink ale gave me the illusion that I was in control of my drinking, when nothing could be further from the truth, not Donald Trump nor any other politician you might care to name.

Two weeks before, I'd realised I was lying on some damp grass, a man's head between my thighs. The man was not my husband. The sky above me was brightening, the birds had started to sing, and I did not know what was happening, only why it was happening. It was happening because I was bad, because I had asked for it, because this man had been feeding me cocaine, and this was clearly how I had chosen to repay him. I lay there, very still, very aware that not even half a mile away, my family lay sleeping in the grounds of the country estate we were staying in to celebrate a friend's fortieth. I did not want the man to be doing what he was doing, but I also felt that I had no right to stop him. So I lay there, and watched as what remained of my soul seeped out into the soil and the trees around me.

Three days after the country house party, back in London, back at work, a strange number had flashed up on the screen of my phone. I was ragged, paranoid, too scared to answer it but also too scared not to. I had entered the final stages of my drinking, the last days of disco, and I was certain that everything and nothing was coming for me. I brought the phone to my ear, and said hello. The man from the fortieth answered back, his voice a haunting I would do anything to exorcise. He said: 'I was wondering if you were still up for that threesome?' And my heart thumped in my chest as I realised two things: that I did not know what he was talking about, and yet somehow also did. I was scared of this person, of how he knew things about me that I did not. I was scared of *all* the people out there in the world who knew things about me that I did not. It was not inconceivable to me that, in my coked-up, crazy state, desperate for more drugs, desperate to keep the 'party' going, I had suggested things I knew I would have absolutely no desire to do in the cold, sober light of day. It was even conceivable to me that in this coked-up, crazy state, I had *wanted* to do this thing that I had absolutely no desire to do in the cold, sober light of day. But I had no memory of it, nor what I had offered other than some variation of group sex. Now I became frantic with worry about what else I might have said and done at this 'celebration' of our mutual friend's significant birthday.

Someone had once told me that drugs and alcohol brought out the real you. Was I this monstrous creature, prostituting herself out for a quick high? And if so, how did I go about cremating her? I had got used to thinking on my feet, at making excuses for this other version of me and justifying her behaviour. Now I was running out of ways to rationalise her, because she was not rational, not at all. She was mad, and bad, and increasingly dangerous to know. She was living on adrenaline and borrowed time and I didn't know how much longer I had before she dragged me down with her. I suspected it was not long, a matter of months at most, before she trashed the strange reputation I had somehow managed to build for myself as a mental health campaigner.

This, then, was the weird juxtaposition of my life: I had never before been so successful but I had also never before felt like such a mess, and I was a woman who had experienced six breakdowns. I was two people in one, having to hide ever more shameful secrets under an increasingly impossible-to-maintain list of professional triumphs. My inbox was filled with people who wanted to tell me how amazing I was. I was keen to reply that I was a fraud. I was the very worst kind of mental health advocate, one seemingly incapable of taking her own advice. 'Get help! Talk to someone about it!' I would parrot, but I could not talk to anyone about this dirty, dark secret I kept inside me.

'You are going to destroy yourself,' my husband had said a few months earlier when I had come home at 9.30 a.m. the day after one of the biggest moments in my career. I had ended up on a bender, in a stranger's house, snogging a woman who was also snorting cocaine off my breasts as her boyfriend looked on. My husband was right. I was going to destroy myself – not to mention him, in the process – and I needed to do it sooner rather than later, so that the collateral damage was smaller.

So, with this man from the country house party still waiting for a response on the phone, I looked for a corner of the office to hide in, so nobody could hear me, and I took a deep breath before apologising to him, and telling him I had not been myself that night. I did not add that I had no idea who myself was, that the boundaries between the two versions of me had blurred to the point of disappearing entirely, if indeed they had ever existed in the first place. The man sounded humiliated, then cross, like I had somehow let him down by turning out to be exactly the kind of person you'd expect someone who scabs cocaine off you to be. He hung up the phone and all I could hear was the sound of my heart thudding in my chest. If ten minutes ago I had been fighting off the lethargy that was the inevitable legacy of a two-day bender, now I was wide awake and alert to danger everywhere. I was surrounded by shame, sitting in shame, subsumed by shame. I had coloured the world in shame. It drove each and every decision I made, and it was slowly corroding me.

*

And now I had left Harry and Edie at home and I was still staring at the conker I had picked up from the pavement on my way to the pub. It felt shocking to me. It felt offensive. I wanted to unsee it. I wanted to unsee almost everything my drinking and drugging had shown me over the years, in particular: the brightness of the sky as dawn broke on another night of drinking; the sight and sound of the birds as they began their coarsely cheerful chorus announcing another day I had managed to fuck up before it had even got going; the normal people going about their business, scurrying around and going to work as if living was *easy*. I didn't realise it then but what I really wanted most of all was to live in the darkness. Or, more accurately, to die in it. I wanted to be unseen. Unseen and undone, as if I had never even existed in the first place.

I dropped the conker back to the ground, tried to stamp on it, to split it open and kill it, but I was only wearing Havaianas and frankly they weren't up to much. I scowled at the conker, as if this, too, were its fault. This fucking conker, I decided, was responsible for the downer that had suddenly swept over my evening. If only I could have smashed it to pieces, if only it hadn't been so obstinate, I would now be feeling footloose and fancy-free and everything would be fine and fucking dandy. This sense of impending doom had absolutely nothing to do with me and *my* actions. No. Not at all.

13

At the pub, I had arranged to meet a friend who was not actually a friend, more like someone who had been in my acquaintance for many years. I knew only two things about her: that she liked to party, and that she always had cocaine on her to help her carry on partying. And this knowledge was enough for me. I would hang around the seediest of people if their behaviour made me feel somehow normal. My world was shrinking, my friends with hobbies and interests jettisoned because they couldn't hack the pace. Or my pace, at least. There were only two or three people I could safely drink around, and one of those people was me. How many nights had I spent alone in the back garden, scrolling idly through Facebook and Twitter as I chugged back beer and fags and bemoaned the fact that my husband wanted to eat dinner and go to bed by ten?

At least when I was in the garden, he knew that I was contained. He knew that in all likelihood, I would shuffle up to bed some time after eleven when I would black out next to him, coming to four or five hours later and prodding him awake to ask if I had behaved badly the night before. 'No,' he would mumble robotically from under the duvet, his answer, at that time in the morning, given to reassure me rather than shed any light on the truth and risk me disrupting yet more of his life. 'You just sat in the garden a bit longer and then came up and fell asleep.' I would frantically go through my phone – my Facebook messages, my WhatsApp, my Instagram posts – to check I hadn't posted or sent anything embarrassing, while he fell back to sleep. My body was too full of panic to rest. What would the neighbours think of me, sitting out there by myself, guzzling back booze? I lived in fear of the neighbours, these soft, quiet people who had never said anything to me other than the odd 'hello', but who my mind had fleshed out to be sitting in almost permanent judgement of me, as if they had nothing better to do with their time.

Sometimes I told my husband – my sweet, kind, patient husband – that I had stayed up to write, or to search for ideas for my next column. We both knew that this was categorically not true, but we had got to the stage where it was just easier to believe the lies than challenge them. The hopeless stage, that is. And I was good at charming him, at manipulating him. I balanced out the darkness by shining on him an almost blinding light, an upbeat charisma that I believed atoned for my sins. Tonight I was out, and it didn't occur to me for a minute that my husband might be worried about me. That he might spend his Friday evening in a state of heightened anxiety, pacing the living room, wondering what I was up to, where I had got to, what situation he was going to have to mop up when he woke up in the morning, if indeed he managed to get himself to sleep. The possibility that I might have destroyed someone else's peace of mind never occurred to me: I was too busy worrying about my own to care about anyone else's. We were where we were, or I was where I was, and as long as that place involved getting out of it then that was all that mattered.

As I approached the pub I could almost convince myself that all of this was totally normal. Me, a 37-year-old woman walking away from her young family to drink herself into oblivion with a person she barely knew. But. But but but. Fuck the buts. My mood lifted – it could veer from one extreme to another in the blink of an eye. The shadows were lengthening but it was still warm and sunny as I approached the pub, which was busy with people sitting on the benches out the front and enjoying the last rays of the day. It was the beginning of the bank holiday weekend, and I could see my 'friend' sitting at one of the tables outside, a bottle of rosé in a bucket of ice next to her. She looked up and waved. I think I looked dispropor-tionately pleased to see her, given that I could not tell you where she lived, or what her surname was, just that she had an Instagram account that mostly featured pictures of her posing next to cocktails larger than her head. I hated cocktails. They were alcoholic drinks for people who didn't often drink alcohol, who saw it as an occasional treat that needed to be turned pink or blue or be decorated with a parasol. Still, this 'friend' – who, now I came to think of it, I had only met on a handful of occasions at parties before I had got pregnant and married – would do. She served a purpose, and that purpose was escaping from my head.

She leapt up and hugged me. 'It is SO good to see you after all this time!' She smiled, held me at a slight distance so she could appraise me and check how much I had altered, which, as I was about to prove, was: not much. 'Look at you! So much has changed since I last saw you! When was it? Ten years ago? No, it must have been seven! You'd just met Harry?' I let myself stew on this. When had I last seen her? Did I even want to remember where that night had ended up, or what I had done? A vague memory began to form in my mind of a neighbour screaming at us to turn the music down, and this girl screaming back and using the word cunt.

I shook it from my head. 'Oh yes!' I let out a chuckle. 'I think we ended up having some crazy party at your flat and the neighbour went mad!'

'That was it!' My friend whose full name I didn't know clapped her hands to her chest. 'Bet those days seem like ancient history to you now you're a mum.' I decided, as I often did, to go along with this charade that I was now a proper grown-up, and really ham up the former party girl who never gets to behave badly any more. People liked it, as it gave them permission to behave badly too: it was all just a bit of fun and we would return to our sensible, real lives the next day. If they were still there, in my case.

'I got us a bottle of rosé,' said my friend, raising the ice bucket aloft.

'That is so sweet of you, but now I'm a bit of a lightweight I can't really drink wine. Would you mind if I went and got myself an ale?'

'Of course not!' My friend smiled a rictus grin. She looked a little alarmed at the prospect that I might now be the kind of person who flaked out after one or two. Though I didn't really know her I still *knew* her. I was her too: a person for whom the only acceptable outcome of a night was oblivion. I would play this to my advantage, of course. By now the drinking part of me had made almost all of me manipulative and sly and self-serving.

At the bar, I ordered myself a pint, and was relieved to see that inside the place wasn't too busy. There was nothing worse than a packed pub with a queue for the bar three deep. No, there was: having to go to a restaurant and count the minutes for the waiter to come back with your drinks order when you knew you could do it quicker yourself. We never went out for dinner any more because of this: the eating got in the way of the drinking and I wasn't interested in it. Sometimes we would have people over for takeaway pizza and champagne, and wear our dysfunction like a glamorous badge of honour. But that was as far as it went. The idea of enjoying a glass of wine at a dinner party appalled me.

The man behind the pumps handed me my ale and asked if I wanted to set up a tab. I smiled knowingly at him, and handed over my card, before turning on my heel and walking back to my friend at the table. Sitting down, I lit a cigarette and took a sip of the ale and I exhaled. I exhaled all the shame, all the feelings of self-loathing. In one moment, they vanished entirely. It was like a form of magic, even if it was actually a form of madness, and it is still evocative enough to bring me to tears all these years later. Safely delivered to this false utopia, I relaxed and decided to go with it. I was here now and absolutely nothing else mattered: not my child or my husband or my tax bill or the fact that a couple of weeks earlier I had allowed a man I had never met before to give me oral sex in return for drugs. In that moment, none of these things would ever matter again, and I lived for this moment; I would die for this moment. Was dying for this moment.

My friend raised her glass and said cheers. I followed suit. 'It is so, so wonderful to be out of the house,' I said, the euphoria of the moment flooding through me. 'So good to have a free pass!' My friend laughed as I humoured her. 'You will not believe how glad I am to see you.' I took a swig of my drink and then feigned restraint. 'I better go steady, don't want to peak too soon.' We laughed, hollowly.

'Oh don't worry,' said the friend I didn't know. 'I have ways of keeping you going.' She winked and smiled. This was code, code for the fact that she had cocaine.

It had been that easy, then, to get in on her stash: I had only had to pretend for a matter of minutes. More euphoria flooded through me. 'Well then, maybe I won't be so sensible this evening.'

'It is the bank holiday, after all,' she said, sloshing more wine into her glass. Right then this woman I barely knew was my kindred spirit. She was my soul mate, and I would have done anything for her, or more pointedly for her cocaine. We drank and reminisced, and she told me again and again how amazing I was, how much she admired me for being so open and honest about my *struggle*. I lapped it up; here, then, was another person willing to partake in the delusion that everything was just fine, that I had won some battle with my mental health and was now enjoying a life of glorious triumph: interviewing royalty, running marathons, watching the book I had written about my struggle become a bestseller.

Eventually I felt her kick my Havaianas in a way that did not seem accidental. I looked at her and she looked towards the table, and I realised that she was subtly trying to hand me her coke. My mood soared as I reached under the wooden pub table and took delivery of the paper wrap. There was a time when coke only came into play late at night, when I could convince myself that I didn't need it and that booze was enough, but my friend and I were both past that point now. I hadn't even finished my pint – though I nearly had – and already I was slipping the gram into my wallet and heading to the loo under the pretence of getting another drink.

In the toilet there were no flat surfaces. The toilet lid had been removed and the cistern had been hidden in an effort to show the police that this pub was serious about cracking down on drug use. I spotted the sanitary bin and briefly considered using it – I was not above this, not at all – but the lid was wedged open by a mass of sanitary towels and I could think of other ways to get my kicks. I sat on the loo and coughed loudly as I reached into my handbag to pull out my wallet and my iPhone. I balanced the phone precariously on my knee, which I willed to stop shaking. I pulled the wrap out of my wallet and searched for my supermarket loyalty card, having long ago stopped using my bank card because it made me feel ill when I saw the powder

21

pressed into the embossed numbers as I went about my normal life, my normal life being the one that involved taking my daughter to buy new shoes. My daughter. I could not think of her now.

I found the card and a rolled-up five-euro note next to it. The five-euro note from a recent trip to Italy that made me feel like a normal mum who does normal things like go on holiday with her family to Tuscany. With all the tools I needed at my disposal, I set to work. I put the note in my back pocket, ready for the moment. That moment. The one I had been waiting for ever since I decided I was going out to drink. I got the card and very carefully used it to coax some of the white powder from the wrap and onto the back of my iPhone. It was crucial that I stayed as still as I could, that I did not drop anything. I placed the card down on my thigh and folded the wrap back up, putting it safely next to the note in my pocket. Then I returned to the powder, crushing it into tiny particles and heaping it into a neat line with the card. Once done, I licked the edges of the card and tasted the metallic tang that lit me up like a Christmas tree. I replaced the card with the note, unfurled it, rolled it back up into a perfect mini straw shape, and then I hunched down over my iPhone and I snorted. I snorted that line up into my right nostril – always my right nostril, for some reason, so that by now its cartilage was worn down – and I let out a high humming sound as I did it, partly to mask the sound of my snorting but partly because I was high and happy, or some approximation of it.

I stood up, dropped the note into my handbag, and flushed the toilet, even though I hadn't actually used it. When I opened the door I was relieved to see that nobody was there. I washed my hands, checked my face in the mirror for any tell-tale signs of powder. None. I smiled at myself, at how clever I was. How wonderful this was. Why didn't everyone do it? Why weren't you told about it at school or by your parents? Why wasn't this shit state-sanctioned? Alcohol and cocaine, the perfect combination, like cheese and onion or sweet and sour or cookies and cream. Man, I was ecstatic. Life was good. No, scrap that, life was great, life was joyous, life was the dancing woman in a red dress emoji. I had even forgotten about the conker.

I strutted back to the table and the grinning face of my friend, who looked fantastic. Really, really fantastic. I told her. 'You look fantastic!' I said, remembering that I had forgotten to buy myself another drink. I didn't sit down. 'Oops, back to the bar!' As I turned I heard my fantastic friend laugh. I remembered the conker, but now it wasn't bad, now I just wanted to talk about it, and how utterly amazing it was to be seeing a conker before the end of August. Or maybe it was bad. I didn't know. I didn't really know anything other than the fact that even if the apocalypse were to happen right now, I'd be fine, because I had a pint of ale, a gram of coke (maybe more?) and my fantastic friend with me.

'I saw a conker!' I exclaimed as I sat back down with my pint.

'No way!' said my fantastic friend. We had already reached the stage of talking in exclamation marks, and it wasn't even 7.30 p.m. 'I love conkers,' remarked my new best friend. 'They're so . . .' She lit a fag. 'So conkery.'

'Yeah, they are!' I also lit a fag. 'And you know, I just LOVE the autumn.' This was a lie. I hated it because it meant that I would have to stop drinking, or I would fail at having to stop drinking and continue drinking, which was worse. 'I just love it when the leaves turn and I can just go for walks and hunker down with my family.' This wasn't a lie, but it certainly hadn't been a truth for some time. But I was warming to my theme, enjoying it even. 'You know, life is so different since I last saw you. So boring. Like, EXCRUCIATINGLY boring.' My friend nodded her head sympathetically. 'And it is so good to be able to just remember who I am, the person I was before all this responsibility and *tedium* got in the way. I just want to thank you for being an amazing friend and not forgetting me. Thank you thank you THANK YOU for still being here for me and giving me the space to be me again.'

I sucked on my cigarette. My amazing friend nodded at me in a way that said 'give me back my cocaine'. I handed it to her under the table and felt a pang of anxiety that I would never see it again, that I would be stuck in this half-cut state for the rest of my life, unable to move forward to the next high. Which was what? More cocaine, more alcohol? A lonely wank in front of some porn? It was like being stuck in an early version of Super Mario Brothers, always trying to over-come some obstacle so you could advance to the next level. It seemed remarkable to me how quickly the sense of elation wore off nowadays, how seamlessly I was able to move from utter bliss to utter despair in the blink of an eye. But I held my nerve. If my friend was anything like me, and it seemed that she was – though I couldn't precisely say why given that I barely knew her – she would be desperate to have someone to party with, the verb 'party' implying that we were somehow having a celebratory time. She would hand the wrap back to me soon enough; I just had to bide my time, the time being only about seven minutes since I had done my last line of coke.

We discussed her latest boyfriend and the conker and climate change and Brexit and quite possibly we solved all these issues. I made more of how nice it was to be doing this, flattering this near-stranger so that I could continue to spend this glorious August evening drinking and taking cocaine with her. What else would I be doing? No, don't answer that: it's a rhetorical question, obviously. I knew there were many other things I could be doing – hanging out with my family, cooking dinner with my husband, making love to him, packing for our weekend away – but my overwhelming need for alcohol and drugs had scribbled out all possibilities other than this one. The seconds and the minutes and the hours ticked by, seconds and minutes and hours of my one, precious life that I would never get back, like so many other seconds, minutes and hours of it. Gone, vanished, no accounting for how or where they were spent, nor, often, with whom. I was a ghost, haunting my own life. I had disappeared on myself.

I was aware of texts from Harry, checking in on me as if he were my father, not my husband. Or perhaps a carer. How was I doing? Would I be coming home soon? He had cooked some food if I fancied it. Right. He was going to bed, in the spare room, as he had to be fresh to drive, but he had left me some glasses of water on the bedside tables in our room for when I came home. I replied 'cool' and 'thanks' and 'LOVE YOU', and at some point I slunk off to a quiet corner of the street where I called him and exaggerated how

I was totally absolutely fine and not at all off my face and would be home soon. Soon! He didn't believe me, but I convinced myself that he did, and that was all that mattered.

At closing time, my friend suggested we continue the party at her flat, and at this point time became nothing more than an abstract concept to me, something followed by other people, like veganism or Buddhism, a construct created almost purposely to stymie my drinking. At some point, Harry's name began to flash on my phone, my alarm call, my sign that it was time to step back into the real world. I was not ready though, not at all, so I ignored it. The texts began arriving soon after – *where are you, what is happening, you know we have to go to my father's* – and so on and so on, increasingly angry admonishments designed to lure me back to my actual life. I didn't want to go back, though, so I switched off my phone, and continued to snort lines of cocaine and drink whatever dregs my friend had left in her flat.

When I came round, my brain was wrapped in barbed wire and invisible daggers of anxiety were stabbing my stomach and chest. I was on a virtual stranger's sofa, the light flooding in through her living room window and onto her coffee table, highlighting a still life so grim nobody would ever want to paint it. Tobacco; ash; glasses in which diluted whisky had been used to stub out cigarettes. I switched on my phone. Fifteen new messages, the final one sent at 11.30 a.m., which, I see, was two hours ago: *We have gone to Salisbury without you. You do not know the worry you are putting me through. Please call. We cannot go on like this; it is not fair for our daughter to grow up thinking this is normal. H.*

It was the worst text message I have ever received. But it was also, quite probably, the best thing that had ever happened to me.

2

Surrender

People often ask me what my rock bottom was. They want to know when I decided to stop drinking. As if there was one single moment. As if there was an epiphany. As if a light bulb suddenly appeared above my head – hey, that's a real smart idea! – and that was that. Like waking up one morning and deciding that you are going to go for a run, or declutter the spare room, or finally fix the bathroom grouting. Like making a decision and sticking to it is the simplest thing in the world.

Maybe it is for some people. Maybe it really, truly is.

But it isn't for me.

The truth is, I decided to stop drinking almost as

soon as I started. From the moment I first tasted it, I knew that alcohol was going to have a powerful hold over me. It was one of the first things I just *knew*, deep down inside me, like which football team you support or whether you prefer savoury things to sweet. You know, don't you, the moment that you first try alcohol, whether or not this is something you will be able to simply take or leave. And I could do neither. I chose to stuff this knowledge deep down inside me, to drown it under gallons of alcopops, because it's not really the done thing to stop drinking as soon as you've started, and also because I didn't actually *want* to stop drinking. Because despite the lack of control I had over it, I liked drinking. I liked it a lot. I liked the way it finally made me feel like everyone else, the way it allowed me to fit in, the way it felt like firing up your insides.

What I didn't like was how I felt after drinking, and no matter how fuzzy or blurry those feelings were, within them I knew with absolute clarity that alcohol and I did not get on. That, much like my boyfriend at the time who turned on the charm before turning on the abuse, I was very attracted to alcohol despite alcohol being very bad for me. I always knew in my waters that I was going to have to find some way to stop drinking, in some form: I was going to have to stop drinking so *much*; I was going to have to stop drinking spirits; I was going to have to stop drinking wine; I was going to have to stop drinking during the week; or maybe I was going to have to stop drinking on Mondays, Tuesdays and Wednesdays; and then, eventually, after many, many years and many, many iterations of stopping drinking, came the realisation that I was going to have to stop drinking, full stop.

Every time I drank – and I drank all the time – I set out to prove to myself and others the validity of my relationship with alcohol. That it was fine. That we were fine. And every time, or almost every time, I failed. What I am trying to say is that it's difficult to explain why I eventually decided to *actually* stop drinking: it was made up of a million different moments, all leading up to one, some of which I will never, ever know about because I was too drunk to remember them. I made the decision to stop drinking on more mornings than I didn't. Never again, I would say, knowing that whatever had led to this 'never again' would be replaced by something else that would lead to another 'never again' in a few days' time.

Never again.

Again and again and again.

And again.

Was the night that became my last night of drinking any worse than ones that had come before? I don't think so. Had I become exhausted by the effort involved trying to prove I was something I wasn't?

Yes. Maybe. Did I know that this time my attempts to stop drinking might pay off? Not with any certainty, not at all. But what I did know was that if I didn't at least *try*, I was going to cease to exist in any meaningful way. I was going to become a husk, and everything that mattered was going to fall away from me and I was never going to be able to catch it again. I was never going to be able to get it back.

What I knew was this: that if I didn't stop drinking, I was going to die.

I was going to die, either by accident, falling off a balcony or down a flight of stairs or choking on my own vomit. Or I was going to die on purpose, by actively making the decision to kill myself. Or – absolutely worst of all – I was going to die very slowly, by living in only the most literal of senses, my so-called life tiny and toxic, a Groundhog Day of misery and anxiety.

So when people ask me why, I tell them this: that I stopped drinking because I wanted to start living.

That day in August, when I return to my empty home, my insides turned outside and my family gone, it is clear to me that I have reached a rock bottom. Or that I have reached another of my rock bottoms. And that really the rock bottom I am heading towards is death, that ultimate rock bottom that nobody escapes but that I can at least try to avoid reaching prematurely. I know that if I don't try to stop now the rock bottoms will become seedier and seedier, and I am not sure I will live through them. I am not sure I will survive. I am hollowed out by self-loathing, and I do not think that there is enough energy left in me to carry me through another night like this – or, more pointedly, another day like this.

I realise that my head is a bomb, and that I only have a limited amount of time left to make it safe. I am racing against myself. Somehow, I have to cut the right wire so that my brain can be defused. Currently, the green wire and the red wire are mixed up, and they are sending me messages that are wrong, that are lies, that are tangled up and dangerous: if I want to do something, then I probably shouldn't; if I don't want to do something, then I probably should. The clock is ticking down. My time is running out. Any day now, any moment, my brain is going to explode. It is going to go BOOM.

In the bright daylight of the kitchen, my child's drawings pinned to the fridge, her half-eaten bowl of cereal in the sink, the shame seems almost unbearable. This life that my husband has so steadfastly kept going does not belong to me, and I do not deserve it or them, these precious people who are all that is good and decent and right. I feel like an interloper in my own family. I cannot do this any more. I cannot live like this a moment longer. I am a monster, a grotesque creature who has no right to any of this. I am the worst person in the world. Selfish, sick, verging on the satanic. Something violent seems to be flooding through my system, something that leaves me wondering if I can go on. My hands grab for the packet of paracetamol in the cupboard alongside all the other medicines. I slide out the blister pack, count the tablets, and consider my options, tiny as they are. I do not want to die but nor do I want to live like this, and being hospitalised for an overdose will at least replace the shame of being a 37-year-old mum on a cocaine bender. It will say, once and for all, that I am in need of help.

Something stops me. It is something like the last scraps of my self-esteem, the tiny bits I haven't yet destroyed. There is no guarantee that these remnants of self-protection will not have been made extinct the next time, that I won't have destroyed them, too. I cannot risk doing this again. I cannot be so careless with my life. I cannot be so careless with my husband's life, nor my daughter's, with the lives of these people who, against all the odds, still love me. I lay the blister pack down on the kitchen countertop and I switch on my phone and I call my husband. It is not hard for me to do this. It is the easiest thing in the world, in the end. It is a relief, actually, a form of surrender, a tacit acknowledgement that I am no longer capable of looking after myself. He picks up the phone and I sob. I say things like 'I need you' and 'help me', things that I have not ever said before despite telling other people all the time to do this themselves. I need you. Help me. Please.

He tells me it is OK. I tell him it isn't. He tells me it will be. He says he is coming home, that they are coming home, that he will tell his dad that the flu I have has worsened and he thinks it unwise to leave me alone. There are so many lies to untangle, so many layers of denial and deceit: what does another one matter, really? How many times have I had the flu, how many times have I been bedridden with food poisoning? I have lost track. I have forgotten how to speak the language of truth.

I go upstairs, find the pints of water he left the night before on the bedside table. I down them, even though by now they taste stale and old. I have put far, far worse things in my body in my time. I throw off my clothes, soiled with the memories of the night before, and leave them in a pile of shame at the end of my bed. I know I will not sleep of my own accord, that there are too many chemicals still in my body to deliver me anywhere close to rest, so I go back downstairs and into the cupboard and pull out some Night Nurse to knock myself out. It occurs to me that I now spend most of my life knocking myself out, but the thought of being awake and alone for the next three or so hours while they drive back is too awful to comprehend. I cannot be alone with myself. I go into my daughter's room and find one of her stuffed toys that smells like her and then I take it with me into my own bed, hold it to me under the duvet and inhale deeply. I try to breathe all her goodness into me, and then I panic that I have put all my badness into her. I am grateful that my night of shame took place elsewhere, that the sheets in my room are clean and do not hold any remnants of my behaviour. I hold the toy to me and imagine myself in the apocalypse, safe and warm in an underground bunker with my family and all the food and water we need, the end of the world banishing all this to nothingness. This is where I must go to for comfort nowadays: armageddon.

Eventually the Night Nurse and the apocalyptic thoughts soothe me into something approaching sleep, the duvet pulled over my head, my body able to convince itself that it is back in the womb, if the womb belonged to a drug-addicted lunatic. I have come to wonder, in these recent stages of my drinking, if my body ever does anything as nourishing as sleep at all. If my brain doesn't just shut everything down at some point, as a means of survival – stop this human from putting any more poison inside her! – before jolting me awake a few hours later, dry-mouthed and almost dead inside, so I can begin the reparations to myself and others: apologies; promises never to do it again; gallons of water; several different types of vitamins, minerals and supplements; a hot yoga class to sweat out all the toxins.

I come round to the sound of the key in the door downstairs. I am freezing cold, sweat pooled between my breasts, the sheets soaked with the efforts my body has made to cleanse itself while I was passed out in my Night Nurse-induced coma. Usually my brain gives me a brief moment of respite when I wake up after a night out, but not today. The chatter of my husband tending to our daughter downstairs brings the shame straight down on me, as it should. I am rotten. I am wrong. I realise that I have nourished and nurtured my drinking almost as much as I have my own child, the alcohol acting like a demanding older sibling who takes up all my attention. And the worst thing of all is that my daughter has never known anything different. To her, at this tender age, a distracted, hungover mother is absolutely normal. It is my job now to ensure I change that normal before she is old enough to realise how *ab*normal it is.

'Shoes off . . . Let's get a snack and you can watch some TV . . . I'm just going to check on Mummy and then we can go to the park.' In any other house these would be normal things to say on a day like today, the Saturday of the August bank holiday weekend. But here, now, they shock me. They remind me of all that is wrong in my world. I try to sit up. I try to shout 'hello!' in a jaunty, jolly voice, but my body will not allow it. I scurry across the hall to the bathroom and close the door behind me. In the mirror I see a woman with mascara smudged across her face, her eyes rimmed with redness and crusty bits of who knows what. The taste in my mouth no longer repulses me. I am immune to its awfulness, but know it is there. I scrub at my face with make-up remover and water. I floss and brush my teeth, before gargling with mouthwash, the behaviour of someone almost normal.

Harry opens the door. There is fury in his face, and there is never, ever fury in his face. My husband and I are opposites; where I am impetuous and flighty, he is calm and stoical. He is not prone to anger or any other extreme emotion. He is Harry – easygoing, pragmatic Harry. At times it amazes me that we ever ended up together – him, collected and steady, me, loud and garish. But our opposites had very much attracted, and we had drawn from each other a sort of strength via the qualities we lacked in ourselves. We were a unit, we were each other's people, we worked together, and that was that. From the moment I met him six years previously, it had never even occurred to me that we wouldn't be together, a trusty team who found sameness in our differences. But now, in his crestfallen, collapsed face, I saw the threat of our differences splitting us apart.

'I hope that whatever happened last night was worth it,' he manages to say. Tears somehow prick through the numbness in me. He has no time for them. He has seen them all before, been manipulated by them too often. 'You stink,' he says. 'I'm running you a bath and then we can talk.'

I watch as he fills the tub with light green bubble bath, the type my mum used to have when I was a child. I feel very small, very stupid. I am thirty-seven, but my husband is having to run a bath for me. 'Can you make it really hot?' I say, and I flinch even as I ask this, knowing I have no right to demand anything of him at all. He doesn't say anything. He leaves the bathroom and goes downstairs where he affects an air of lightness as he talks to our daughter, who wants to see her mummy. 'Mummy is going to have a bath to make herself feel better,' he explains, 'and while she is having the bath we can go to the park.'

'I don't want to go to the park,' I hear her harrumph. 'I want to have a bath with Mummy.'

'If we go to the park we can get an ice cream.' His voice is sing-songy but also pleading.

'No! No ice cream! I want MUMMY!'

I am toxic and wrong but I am not immune to the cries of my daughter. I go downstairs and Harry looks at me fiercely as I gather her into my arms. She is happy, and then I see that she is, against her wishes, repulsed. 'Mummy, you smell,' she almost laughs, registering that something is not quite right in this situation. She is young, but she is not stupid, and she is absorbing this situation into her brain without even realising it. How long before it starts to change the very fabric of her cells, of her story, damaging her until there is no going back?

'I know!' I try to beam. 'Mummy has been sick so needs to have a bath so she doesn't smell any more. So why don't you go to the swings and then when you're back we can hang out and watch a movie? Maybe we could even go to the toy shop!' I know, as soon as I say this, that I cannot go to the toy shop, that I will not make it out of the house today, that it is Harry who will have to take her to the toy shop to buy her the gift I am using to win her affections with. But I am swept up in the moment, and can see her smiling. 'OK, Mummy,' she says. 'That sounds good.' I hold her to me tightly, and imagine never letting go.

I go back upstairs and get in the scorchingly hot bath and listen as my family go through the motions of getting ready to go to the park. Inside me there is a dark, rotten void and I cannot foresee a time where I will ever again go through the motions of getting ready to go to the park, where this will just be a thing that happens on a weekend, bright, breezy, *normal*. The water stings my skin but the pain is satisfying, deserved. I slink under the water and briefly consider not coming back up, but I am too lumbering and big for the bath to stay there. I do not belong, even in the bath. My husband and daughter leave the house. All is still and quiet.

I scrub my body. I cover every inch of it with shower gel. I shave all the hair off my armpits and legs, as if these hairs somehow contain the shame of the previous night. I shampoo my hair once, twice and then thrice to make sure that whatever coated it last night is gone. I get out of the bath and wrap myself in my towelling robe, then I spray on deodorant, brush my hair, my teeth again, put on a pair of leggings, a T-shirt and a jumper. It is warm outside, and I burn with shame, but I am also cold, so cold. I get back under the duvet and text my husband to tell him I've cleaned up and then I find I have to get back out of bed and do something because when I lie still and flat I am swamped with all the feelings that come from being me.

I text my 'good' friend and thank her for a great night out, my stomach churning as I tap out the words, my intentions manipulative even now: I have no interest in thanking her, really, just in checking that I didn't do anything bad in her company, or anything *else* bad, above and beyond the common-or-garden badness that is staying up all night taking cocaine and drinking when you should be at home with your family. Almost immediately, I can see that the message has been read, but there are no tell-tale dots to let me know she is replying. The daggers come back, flooding my body and my brain with the catastrophic possibilities of all the things I might have done. No scenario is too outlandish, no theory too wild. Perhaps I tried to kiss her. Perhaps I smashed her favourite picture frame. Perhaps I announced my intentions to murder my family, and her family, too. Perhaps she was currently calling the police, who would shortly be on their way to get me. Perhaps, perhaps, perhaps. My life had entered such a hazy state that I could not with any conviction tell the difference between what was and wasn't true, the OCD I had experienced since childhood now such a warped and dangerous beast that it was hard to know where I ended and it began.

It is unbearable. I am unbearable. A message pops up on my screen. I grab the phone, hoping to see my friend's name and feel relief, but instead there is Harry's name, above a message telling me they will be home from the park in an hour. An hour! I feel despair, then anger that it is a text from my husband and not this almost-stranger I will almost certainly never see again. I do not know what to do with myself. I pace the hall, put last night's clothes in the wash, having briefly considered burning them. I decide that I will masturbate, masturbation having long been my go-to activity to help change the way I feel. That will pass some time. That will take me out of this grotesque situation I seem to have catapulted myself into. I march upstairs and set about making myself come, and then I do it again and again and again until I once more hear the key in the lock, the metal clank being just the passion killer I need to take me away from this make-believe world where nothing is wrong and life is one long orgasm. As the sensation ebbs away I feel disgusted with myself; with the realisation that even while I have caused my family so much pain, my only thought is of seeking pleasure.

The thought brings me to my knees.

Over my sobbing I can just about hear my daughter shouting, 'We're home, Mummy, we've got you lunch!' Her innocence makes me sob more. I hear footsteps coming up the stairs and when I look up my husband and child are above me, 'What's wrong, Mummy, are you OK?' coming from her mouth and 'Shh shh shh, it's going to be OK' from his. He rubs my back and I realise, as I feel her arms around me, that I am being comforted by my four-year-old daughter. This tiny person who is supposed to look to me for support is instead providing it for me. She jumps down and goes to her room and returns with a plastic doctor's kit. She puts the toy stethoscope round her neck and says to me, 'Now, patient, what seems to be the matter today? Let me check your heart!' Then she places the toy stethoscope approximately where a four-year-old might think your heart is, and I wonder: if this were a real stethoscope, what would she hear right now? Would there be anything there? Just my love for her and her father, the love that hasn't been poisoned by my drinking.

A conversation, that night.

Me: I am a bad person.

Harry: You are not a bad person. You are just an ill person who sometimes does bad things.

Me, asking myself the question I have never dared to ask: Do you think I am an alcoholic?

Harry, nodding slowly: Yes. Yes I do.

It surprises me, how relieved I am to hear him say this. How much those words sound like safety to me. For there is no unsaying things like that. There is no turning back now. I must go into the forgiving arms of my person, and I must never again take them for granted.

*

My drinking wasn't always like this.

Occasionally, very occasionally, it was worse. Far, far, worse.

But sometimes – most of the time, in fact – it was *fine*. And by fine, what I mean to say is that the consequences of my drinking mostly took place only in my own head, which was not fine, not at all – it was dark, ugly, paranoid, exhausting. But the drinking itself: well, that was monotonous, tedious, boring. It took place in my living room, and if the weather was nice my garden. Sometimes I went to the old man's pub round the corner, dressing up these forays with my husband as 'date nights', so that the nanny wouldn't baulk at how often we went on them, and would instead see it as a normal part of a loving relationship. Where did she think we went? Out for dinner? To the theatre? I could tell that my husband would *rather* have done this, but like most people who live with alcoholics, he had had to learn to be accommodating.

Cocaine had only become a regular feature of my nights in recent weeks, though this implies that I didn't in some way have previous with it. I did. Drugs had played a huge part in my twenties, but I had abandoned them the moment I found out I was pregnant, convinced a life of sophisticated occasional red wine drinking lay ahead of me, and that the sordid, chaotic part of my existence was done and dusted. But I was realising that

I had not left the drugs behind: I had merely managed to outrun them for a while. Now they were catching up with me again, their ability to sober me up and keep me drinking making them an increasingly appealing prospect. No matter that they also bankrupted me morally and led me into dangerous situations and did all sorts of awful things to the organs in my body: all that concerned me was that they continued to give me the illusion I was in control of my drinking, at least *while* I was drinking. There was no doubting how beyond it I was the rest of the time, and if it seems strange to you that I should carry on even with this knowledge and certainty inside me then congratulations: you are not and probably never will be an alcoholic. All I know is that I am, in some strange way, eternally grateful for the misery that cocaine delivered me, for how visibly grim it made things. Without it, how long would I have stayed out there living that miserable, fuzzy, hungover excuse of a life?

These 'fine' drinks I speak of – the normal ones in the garden, or at pubs with friends, the ones that didn't end in cocaine binges and sexual deviance or disappearing on my husband – these, I realise, were the most dangerous drinks of all. They were the ones that allowed my drinking to occupy some strange hinterland where denial grew in abundance, where I could convince myself that everything was OK. It was just bad enough to make me want to read books like this, but seemingly not quite as bad as the things I read in books like this. I didn't drink in the morning, unless of course I was still up from the night before (a twice or thrice or perhaps four times a year event), and I didn't drink every day – just every other day. I had never hidden booze in garden hedges, nor woken up and had a drink, nor been hospitalised because of alcohol, nor lost a job, a husband, the roof over my head.

Not yet, anyway.

But on the other hand, I did do things like: hide where I had been, and who I had been with; wake up and take a diazepam so I could immediately go back to sleep and block out the day; fantasise about being hospitalised for 'exhaustion', so I could be sedated; frequently lose my dignity, my soul, my sense of who I was.

My life had come to be defined by alcohol. I thought about it even when I wasn't drinking it. *Especially* when I wasn't drinking it. It was all well and good that I didn't drink every day, but what did any of this matter if I *thought* about drinking every waking moment of the day? I could tell myself that I was not as bad as the person who drank morning, noon and night, but given that I was obsessing about drinking morning, noon and night, was that even true? My drinking structured my whole week. If I had an important work meeting on a Tuesday, that meant I couldn't drink on Monday, which meant I had to drink on Sunday. If I had a party to go to on Wednesday, that meant I couldn't schedule in any important work on Thursday. And so on.

These rules – never drink before 7 p.m., or in front of your child – were very important to me, because they proved I wasn't an alcoholic. And sometimes, it felt as if my entire life's work was proving that I wasn't an alcoholic. Of course, the effort I expended doing this probably should have told me that I absolutely *was* an alcoholic, but I could not bear the word and would have done anything to avoid it. It conjured up images of tramps on park benches, of the destitute and desperate, and I was none of these things. Well. I was only one of these things: desperate. But I couldn't be an alcoholic, I just couldn't, because my career was thriving and I had a house and a mortgage and a husband and a child and expensive blonde highlights and I had written books and run marathons and I don't know if I've mentioned it, but I had once interviewed Prince Harry. Me! An alcoholic? No.

But just to be sure, I often did those online quizzes that had been created to help people know if they were drinking sensibly or not. OK, maybe they weren't quizzes – maybe that kind of suggests that there was an element of fun to them. Maybe they were more like questionnaires. Whatever they were, I didn't need them to tell me that I was not drinking sensibly, that I had never drunk sensibly. And yet . . . surely there was a difference between not drinking sensibly and being an alcoholic? A huge, gaping difference! I mean, sure, I often found that once I started drinking I couldn't stop, and I sometimes failed to do what was expected of me because of my drinking, and I frequently experienced guilt and remorse after drinking, but then . . . didn't *everyone*? Wasn't that the very point of drinking? And didn't they know that as well as drinking well over my weekly allowance of units in one night, I also ran and ate well and sometimes did Reformer Pilates? Surely this counted for *something*?

I was very good at making my drinking look fun. Really very good. In my twenties, I would take all the bad things that happened to me on a night out and turn them into hilarious anecdotes, as if me making pithy judgements about myself would stop other people from doing the same thing. My employers, who happened to be a newspaper, loved this, and gave me a party girl column. So now drinking became my career, and my personality, and I had everyone fooled, but also nobody, all at the same time. I was hiding my dysfunction in plain sight, and most people liked this because it made them feel less mad.

But sometimes people saw through it. I was twenty-seven when someone first suggested to me that I might be an alcoholic. That someone was my boyfriend at the time, who also happened to be married with three children. I could not believe what I was hearing. I could not bear the moral posturing from this man who fucked me then returned to his five-bedroom home in the leafy suburbs of North London. How *dare* he? I was a single girl who could do what she liked, even if doing what she liked included frequently drinking until blackout and sometimes, occasionally, sending him twenty-five plaintive text messages in a row. So I dumped him, and moved onto a new boyfriend, who also happened to be married with kids – but on the plus side, *this* married boyfriend cared about me even less, and subsequently never made any judgements about my morally questionable behaviour, just so long as it continued to include me blowing him in Green Park after sundown. I was fine. I was not an alcoholic. Did I mention I did Reformer Pilates? Clearly everything in my life was tickety-fucking-boo!

I frequently tried not to drink, and alcoholics didn't do that, did they? They never wanted to stop drinking – that was the very point of being an alcoholic, wasn't it? And I wanted to stop drinking, all the time. Or at least I wanted to cut down. To be able to moderate. MOD-ER-ATE. Was there a word in the English language I loathed more? 'It's all about moderation,' friends would shrug, when we discussed the guilt of being out all the time. 'As long as I take it easy and only have one or two, it doesn't matter all that much.'

I nodded along sagely. Yes. Quite. But in reality, I had no real idea of what they were talking about. It was like being back in physics class at school. I knew that what they were saying was factually correct, but I had no actual grip on *why* it was so. I could never quite wrap my brain around it. And I tried, oh I tried. I tried drinking a glass of water between each drink, and then alongside each drink, until my bladder begged me for forgiveness and I was physically forced to give up on this idea. I tried putting ice in my wine, to water it down, but instead it just made it more drinkable. I tried slowing my drinking, but that didn't work – I could not alter my drinking speed to anything other than 'person who has been lost in a desert for sixty-five days' speed. So then I tried giving up wine. Wine was the problem, not me. I moved on to beer, and realised that much the same happened with strong continental lager, so then I moved on to session ales, which did just what they said on the tin. I went to Holland and Barrett and bulk-bought shots of things that promised to remove your hangover. I took three times the recommended dose. But I was not an alcoholic. I was not, I was not, I was not.

Once, I did Dry January. I made it to the fifth day, and only because my hangover from New Year's Eve was so bad that it took me that long to recover (I woke up to find boot prints on my knickers. That still makes me feel nauseous to this day). Another time, I told everyone I had got through the whole of Dry January, but the reality was that this was only because I allowed myself a 'cheat' day once a week. Which is to say, I didn't get through the whole of Dry January, not at all.

I tried eating bananas, as a friend had suggested. This friend was one of those people who was able to drink heavily and nonchalantly and yet still know when to call it a night. One minute he would be banging back the whiskey and the cocaine, the next he would be telling me it was 1 a.m. and time to go to bed. How did people like him do this? When had he installed his off switch, and where could I get one too? 'Just have a banana and buck up,' he would say the next day at work, sidling off to the gym, as I lay weeping on the floor, my hangover now a full-blown existential crisis. But bananas didn't work for me in the way they worked for him. All the potassium in the world couldn't save me from myself.

Another time, my boss at work asked if I wanted to write a health feature on quitting drinking through hypnotherapy. Looking back, I realise this was code for: 'I think you need help.' But I didn't need help. No, I didn't. Not at all (*Please, help me!* I blinked). I went along, for shits and giggles, ostensibly, but really because I was intrigued to see if giving up drinking could actually be as simple as that. I reclined in the hypnotherapist's chair and listened to her instructions with my eyes shut for an hour, and guess what? It wasn't. That night, I went to the pub, and necked back five pints of Staropramen. Still, at least I had tried.

Once, when I was about twenty-nine, my mum came round for a pre-planned visit I had forgotten about. I had not been to bed for two days, and was crying. I said to her: 'I think I might need to go to rehab,' and those words were so shocking for both of us that we shook them off almost as immediately as they had been said. It seemed somehow easier that way.

Shortly after that, I bought a *Gardening for Beginners* book on Amazon, because I thought gardening might mean I could not be an alcoholic.

I did Reformer Pilates. I could not be an alcoholic.

I signed up to do a marathon. I could not be an alcoholic. The training regime would stop me from drinking. At least while I was actually running the marathon.

Once, in 2016, just before my second book came out, I found myself at an Alcoholics Anonymous meeting in my lunch break. I had googled the organisation after an accidental bender, and had popped along in my lunch break. Just to see. Just to check that I wasn't what I feared I was. You know. Just to be *sure*. Then the book was published. It was hugely successful, it got to number one, and these things proved that I could not be an alcoholic.

But nobody ends up in a twelve-step meeting by accident, unless they have taken a wrong turning to the church choir.

Which I had not.

By 2017, I found I had started to make friends with people who happened to have got sober. I kept meeting them, at work events or through friends of friends. Instead of being appalled by their sobriety, I was intrigued by it. I wanted to know more. I wanted to see how they had done it. Had it been easy? Was life OK without booze? Did they really never want a drink? And I liked these people who happened to have got sober. I instinctively warmed to them. I felt as if they got me, as if they understood the obsessive intensity I seemed to apply to absolutely everything, from alcohol to work to relationships. It was just a hunch, just an inkling, but I felt as if they were on my wavelength. So I started collecting these people who happened to have got sober, as if they were Pokémon.

In May of that year, shortly after I had completed the marathon and realised that, if anything, my drinking had ramped up as I trained, I found myself experiencing one of my first rock bottoms. My husband was away for the weekend, and I was supposed to be taking Edie to a literary festival at which I was appearing, but it was a glorious Friday, and when a friend texted suggesting she come round for a drink, I decided that Edie and I would get on the train the next morning. We would still make it with plenty of time. I put Edie to bed in my customary fashion: hurriedly, finding the shortest book possible to read, a dummy in her mouth to soothe her despite the fact she was now four, and then I went downstairs and opened the fridge, which almost exclusively contained bottles of beer and chilled cava.

I opened one of the bottles of cava, and went to sit in the warm garden, where I lit a cigarette and exhaled into the glorious release. Ten minutes later, I poured another glass, and my friend turned up, a friend of hers I had not met before tagging along. I suppose this might have annoyed someone else, a person who had perhaps expected a deep and meaningful catch-up. But I was not that kind of person, and as far as I was concerned, the more the merrier.

Within an hour, the person I had not met before had put in a call to her dealer. It shocks me now to think how quickly, in the end, I broke one of my most unbreakable rules: a virtual stranger in my house ordering drugs as my child slept upstairs. I was protected by my privilege, by my middle-class professionalism – and though this line in the sand was crossed only once, I now see that once could have been enough for some involvement from social services. I can barely force myself to type this, but I need to put it all down, because it pierces the wall of denial that can still come up, even now, even this far into sobriety. My problem wasn't that bad, my brain still says. And yet and yet and yet.

At 4 a.m., I texted my agent to tell her I had a stomach bug and would not make the literary festival. God, I was such a genius! Three hours after that, I found myself trying to get to sleep as my daughter woke up. I pulled out my husband's iPad and put on some movies for her as I tried to get some rest. I gave up. I called my mum, and told her we were coming round as I was ill. I ordered a taxi I couldn't really afford, and bundled us in, panic battling it out with utter despair. We had to stop on the way so I could buy water and be sick. In the checkout queue, holding my daughter's hand and watching the normal, happy families going about their Saturdays, I began to cry silently so my child could not see.

That day, at my mum's, I called on one of my Pokémon.

*

They took me to another twelve-step meeting, at which I sobbed throughout. For thirty-five awful, torturous days, each one of them feeling like a year, I managed not to drink. I wept through every one of these days at some point or other; the early elation that I was trying to get sober quickly blunted by the reality of actually trying to get sober. I had told Harry that we should carry on as normal – carry on going out, carry on having people round for drinks in the garden – because I needed to get these hurdles out the way and, what was more, I didn't want to disrupt his life with my attempt at getting sober.

I laugh at this now – I was disrupting his life by *not* attempting to get sober – but I think I was still in a sort of denial; I still could not believe that I was an alcoholic, and still wanted to believe that everything would go away if I could just stop drinking for a bit. I think I imagined that the alcohol would leave my system and everything would start to level out – that some long drowned-out hormone in my body would reappear from the receding sea of booze and I would suddenly come to my senses. But as the sea of booze receded, *everything* else seemed to reappear and get louder: my OCD, my anxiety, the endless worrying that had caused me to drink in the first place. Without the alcohol, and with barely any enthusiasm for the twelve-step program, I had nothing to deal with those anxieties: just me, naked and alone.

Then I went with my husband to a wedding in Italy and I fell off the wagon. Of course I did. What had I expected to happen? It wasn't spectacular. It was a few beers and half a bottle of champagne, and when I woke up in the morning I was hit with that familiar feeling of failure, of once again not managing to do something I had set out to do. I could not bear feeling like this every morning – every time I woke up a little bit of my self-worth died – so I made a decision there and then that I would simply have to give up giving up drinking. I needed to embrace booze, accept it, go with it: I had to stop trying to be something I wasn't. I would be one of those lush ladies you read about in novels, one of Truman Capote's swans, fabulous and well oiled at all times. Yes, *that* was my problem: I was too uptight about drinking, too anxious about it, and if I was going to do it, I might as well do it properly.

I made the mistake of meeting my Pokémon friend for a coffee on my return from the wedding. I wanted to explain to her what I had realised. I wanted to let her know that I was different to her, in some way, that I had managed to find the magic solution to all this pain and angst. She looked at me with something approaching pity, and it cut straight through me like a knife and I burst into tears. Then she picked up her phone, made a call, and told me she was taking me to see her therapist, who happened to be based in a rehab just round the corner and who had five minutes now to see me.

I was floored by what she had done. Angry, if I'm honest. I felt ashamed, humiliated – precisely, I suppose, as you are supposed to feel when someone stages an intervention. But I still got up and followed her, something in me curious to see what would happen, curious to hear what this man would have to say. Maybe he would pardon me, and tell me I had the right idea with this whole embrace-drinking attitude. Maybe he would let me off the hook, and I could go home and chalk this all up to experience, a funny period of my life where I was really, really het up for no reason and just had to stop taking myself so seriously.

The rehab was in a house down a side street. It didn't look anything like I imagined a rehab would. There were no gates, no security guards, no howling people trying to escape. Just a couple of blokes chain-smoking in a small group by the door. So far as I could tell, this ordinary-looking house did not hide a swimming pool or a spa or any of the other things I had come to assume were part and parcel of rehabilitation centres. I was not so naïve as to believe that rehabs existed only as a sort of alternative world to nightclubs for the rich and famous, but even so, I had expected something a little less nondescript than this – a beige house on a cobbled street in a smart part of London next to a vintage car dealership. Pikachu said 'hi' to the smoking men, who I now realised were more like boys, and rang the doorbell. A tall man in jeans and a T-shirt opened the door and said a cursory hello to Pikachu before waving us into the hall. I could tell he was preoccupied, busy. 'This is your friend,' he said, looking at me and smiling, and then: 'Come with me. I don't have long but we can have a little chat in here.'

'In here' was a small room filled with boxes of tissues and chairs. He motioned for me to sit down, and then took his place in front of me. Before he could say a word, I started to cry again. I could tell that this was very normal for him, despite being nothing of the sort for me. He asked me to explain why I was here, and I could not answer his question. 'I don't know if I even should be here,' I said. 'But if I don't have a problem, then why does it feel like I have, all the time?' I began to explain the events that had led me to this nondescript chair in this nondescript house. He nodded as I spoke. When I had finished, he leant forward.

'It sounds like you have alcohol use disorder,' he said, and I liked what he was saying, because it sounded quite medical, it sounded like something one step up from being an alcoholic, something that could probably be solved with a little bit of therapy, me finding at the end that I could drink sensibly after all.

'Some people do mature out,' he continued, catching

me by surprise. 'They drink and use in the way you do, and then they get to their thirties and they just stop.' I see a glimmer of hope in his words. 'But I think you're probably beyond that now, given that you're ...?'

'Thirty-seven,' I whispered.

'Thirty-seven,' he nodded. 'Yep, definitely beyond that.'

Then he said something that took my breath away, something that winded me.

'The thing is, addiction is a lift going down. You can choose to get off at whatever floor you want, but if you get back on, you will go lower. It will get worse. And with situations like yours, there are really only two options available to you: you can either stay in the lift in active addiction, or get out and into recovery from it.'

I could not believe what I was hearing. Me? An addict? I thanked him for his time and went home via the supermarket, where I bought six large bottles of Peroni, stuffing them in my backpack as if I was stock-piling for something. My own personal apocalypse, perhaps.

The night after my August bank holiday all-nighter with the fake friend, as I lay in bed with my husband, our daughter sleeping between us, I realised that I was laying waste to my life and the lives of my family. I realised that it could always be like this: us together, cocooned with one another, instead of us apart, me carousing with strangers as my daughter and husband wondered where on earth I was. It was time to get serious. I could not think of one single hobby or interest I had other than going to the pub. I could not think of anything I enjoyed that didn't involve drinking. Surrounded by my beautiful family, I saw that this was like being offered caviar and choosing instead to eat chips.

'I'm sorry,' I said, for what must have been the six-hundredth time that day. 'I'm sorry I'm such a bad person.'

My husband put his arm around me. 'You're not a bad person,' he sighed, for what must have felt to him like the seven-hundredth time today. 'You're just an ill one who sometimes does bad things.' I was staggered by his continued kindness in the face of such cruelty.

'I think I should go to rehab,' I say.

He nods. Rehab. *Rehab*. I rolled the word around in my mouth like a Polo.

A few days afterwards, I meet my Pokémon friend for a coffee. I apologise to her: for being useless, for being a flake, for taking advantage of her kindness in taking me to twelve-step meetings and then continuing to drink. 'Bryony,' she says. 'You know I did all of these things too? This is what we do when we are ill. And this,' she says, reaching over the table and taking my hand, 'is what we do when we are better. We help people who are going through the things that we went through.'

'I just . . .' I am touched by all this compassion. If only I had a bit of it for myself. 'I really, *really* want to stop drinking,' I manage to say. 'But I don't know if I can.' The thought of it is so unfathomable that I start to cry again.

'I know,' she comforts. 'I know, it was the same for me. But I managed it.'

'Really? Did you really feel this bad? I just look at you and think, "There is no way she could have had a problem like this." You are so calm and collected and I cannot imagine you falling down drunk.'

'But I used to, all the time,' she says, eyes glistening. 'I used to do that and a whole lot worse. It got dark. Really, really dark. So dark that there were points that I thought that the only option left to me was to black out and join the darkness permanently. But I did it, and if I can do it, you can too.' She pauses, and I see that she is crying. 'Bryony, I'm not going to lie and tell you that there is a magic cure for this. If I could give you a pill that would make everything better immediately I would. There is no easy way out of this. But there is a way out, and if you head towards it, you can get through it. I promise, you can. And I also promise that even though it may not seem it right now, all is well, my darling. All. Is. Well. My. Darling. This is where you are supposed to be. And this will bring you gifts you can't even begin to imagine at the moment.'

I look at her. How can she say this? How can she comfort me like this, when I have behaved so heinously, when everything feels like it is falling in around me?

'I don't want to feel like I am feeling right now ever again,' I sob.

'You don't ever have to,' says my actual, real friend. 'You don't have to. If you make the choice not to pick up a drink, you never have to feel like this again.'

3

Lucky me

It is the very beginning of September, and I am back in the nondescript room in the nondescript building sitting on a nondescript chair, and the man from a few months ago is telling me and Harry that this – this period of crushing self-loathing, suffocating anxiety and suicidal thoughts that have dogged me ever since I came home from my last night out just a few days ago – is a 'real window of opportunity'. 'It's a golden moment,' he says, with absolute sincerity.

It's an interesting take on what feels like the worst mental health crisis I have had in my life, but I can see what he means. Any day now, I am going to hit the danger point, the point where the chemicals will have left my body and I will start to feel physically better and the mad voice in my brain will begin to tell me that actually it is all OK, and I have been making a fuss about nothing. Of course I can have a drink! What is life without one! Or two or three or four or eighteen? But I know this is lunacy. The very epitome of madness: doing the same thing again and again and expecting a different result. It has to stop, before I land myself in a . . . well, what, exactly? A rehab centre?

The man has asked me a series of questions to check my eligibility for rehab. There is only one I don't answer 'yes' to, and that is 'do you need a drink in the morning?' The very idea horrifies me. 'God, no!' I shout.

'Not *yet*,' says the man, who has himself once been an active alcoholic. 'This is a progressive illness, and as time goes on you tend to find yourself crossing lines you once could never have imagined crossing.' I think back to that night in May when I stayed up drinking and drugging as my child slept above me, and I swallow back nausea. 'There was a point in my drinking where I could never imagine reaching for a four-pack of Stella in the morning, but that's where I found myself.'

I do not mention that I have drunk in the morning when I have still been up from the night before.

For the princely sum of almost £8,000, I can start at this rehab centre on their outpatient programme almost immediately. I do not have £8,000, of course. What do they take me for? An alcoholic, or a sensible person with savings? I live on my overdraft, and then when I max out that I live on a credit card, before pay day starts the whole insane circle again. But there is, bleakly, nothing that the NHS can really do for me. The taxes I pay out of that overdraft will only help me if my liver fails, or my heart or my lungs or any other part of my body, it seems, except for my mind. My company probably has medical insurance that I could, in some way, call on to get me a residential rehab place at somewhere like the Priory, but I feel too much shame to ask them, and I am convinced I have brought this on myself. Why should anyone else have to bail me out? So sure, £8,000 is a lot of money, but I am desperate, and alcohol is going to end up costing me a lot more than that if I carry on drinking it.

'I think we should see this in investment terms,' says my husband, ever practical. How could two such different people have ended up together? And how have we stayed together? Me, with this man who counts pennies and can just have one drink? It is nothing short of miraculous that he is sitting here next to me, thinking of things in a pragmatic way while I dissolve into a puddle next to him. 'Yes, this is more money than we actually have, but in the long term, it will pay off.'

The rehab man agrees with him. But Harry has some more considerations, to work out once and for all if this is an investment instead of a gamble. 'Can you tell me what your success rates are in terms of getting people sober?' I look at him and feel a flash of annoyance that he should be so practical at a time that is so emotional – and then I feel relieved that I have this capable man next to me to ask the questions I am too out of it to ask.

'It's about normal for a rehab centre,' says the man. 'Around 40 per cent of our clients are still sober six months after leaving. Addiction is a tough illness to manage, I am afraid.' I swallow hard. The odds are not good, but I admire his honesty, and I have always liked a challenge. I look at my husband's kind face, at the worry in his eyes. And I know then that I am going to try to be part of the 40 per cent.

We apply for a loan that morning.

A memory, of the first time I drank. I was fourteen. My friend Emma and I had managed to get our hands on a litre bottle of cider and a 35-centilitre bottle of vodka. I remember the amounts so clearly, if little else. How had we got hold of them? Had we stolen them from parents? Doubtful. They were the cheap types, nothing posh like Smirnoff or that Kopparberg stuff you get nowadays, so we must have somehow managed to buy them from the local offie, even though we were well underage.

We slipped across the road to a park bench. How

funny, that I spent much of my adult life telling myself I was not a park bench drinker, when in fact this is exactly where my drinking had started. It was the very first place it existed. I remember the rancid sweetness of the cider followed by the shocking sharpness of the vodka. I remember that after a bit, Emma stopped, saying she felt woozy. I remember that I felt woozy too, but that the wooziness in itself did not seem like a good enough reason to stop. If anything, it felt like a reason to carry on. The more I knocked back, the more likely I would be to pass through some imagined point where the wooziness would vanish and the buzz would return.

I remember carrying on, until there was nothing left in either bottle, and then I remember vomiting all over my shoes. I remember the yellow bile on my white plimsolls. I remember Emma calling her mum. I remember her mum coming to get us, and putting me in a bath. I remember begging her not to tell my parents, and I remember knowing that she would even though she said she wouldn't.

And I remember that the next weekend, I was out doing it all over again.

I think at first my parents hoped it was just a phase. And then I think my parents hoped it was just the normal behaviour of a twentysomething enjoying herself in the hurly burly media world of London. And then I think my parents hoped that it was just an occasional thing I did to let off steam now that I was a mum. And then . . .

And then they are sitting in my garden one Thursday in early September as Harry prepares the barbecue and I prepare to tell them that I am going to rehab.

'I'm an alcoholic,' I say to them. My dad is drinking a small stubby bottle of beer, the type I never go near because it is too embarrassing to get through an entire crate in under three hours. My mum has a glass of prosecco, the type I never go near because it is far too sweet and I drink it like pop. This is another one of the things that keeps me from thinking I have a problem: surely alcoholics aren't so damn picky?

There is a short silence, a collective intake of breath. My parents are not good at putting on a united front, given that they were divorced fifteen years ago.

'Well yes,' says my mum, politely, smiling, nodding her head emphatically. 'I think you probably are.'

'Now steady on, Jane,' says my dad, who is now looking at their drinks as if they are the elephant in the garden, which of course they are. 'Let's not get too carried away!'

'It's too late for that, Dad,' I snap. 'I have already been carried away and now I am way out to sea waiting for the lifeboat to come and get me.'

'I think it's good you can still master an arresting metaphor, even in the darkest times,' says my mum cheerfully.

'Anyway, I'm going to rehab. I can start on Tuesday. Harry and I have decided it's the—'

'Rehab!' says my father. He takes a large gulp of his beer and nods towards Harry, motioning for more. 'Blimey, it *must* be bad.'

'It is,' I say, with a rictus grin.

'Well, whatever we can do to support you, just let us know!' My dad has processed the information, and in typical Dad fashion, it appears he is ready to move on. 'As long as it doesn't involve getting us to pay for it, obviously.' He laughs at his own joke. 'Well I never,' he says, taking another long sip from his beer. 'Rehab! I could never do that, you know, never. I have to have my beer every night. Just one bottle, mind – I never like more than that, I don't like to lose control – but I couldn't give that one bottle a night up. Seven o'clock rolls round and I'm straight to the fridge for my—'

'JACK!' bellows my mother. 'I do not think this is helping. I think Bryony probably finds it very hard to have just one beer, don't you, darling?'

'You can say that again,' I mutter. 'And as for the drugs—'

'One thing at a time, Bryony,' says my dad, his nostrils flaring and eyes popping. 'One thing at a time.'

'Will it be like the type of rehab centre where you are locked away with celebrities?' My mum likes to ask the questions that matter.

'No, I don't think so, Mum,' I say. 'It's outpatient. It's more like going on a three-month course. I will go along two nights a week and every Saturday and it means Edie will think everything is normal.'

'Well, that's good,' says my dad. 'Apart from the celebrity bit, obviously.'

'JACK!'

'Don't pretend you're not disappointed, Jane!'

'About the celebrities or the fact I'm going to rehab?' I am fuming. 'GOD, I'M SORRY FOR EVEN MENTIONING IT!' I am thirteen again. Harry pokes the barbecue, pretending he is too busy to have heard the exchange. I get up and storm to the living room to check on Edie, who is watching *Peppa Pig*. My mother follows me through, puts a conciliatory arm around me, and tells me she is proud of me. I stare sullenly at the TV in silence, stroking my daughter's back and wondering what horrors await me in a decade or so's time.

My parents were very bohemian. *Are* very bohemian. They met, ironically, when they were both working for a drug-addiction charity, where my mother was a receptionist and my father campaigned to get the organisation more funding. Neither of them had any personal history of addiction; they were both just bleeding heart liberals who believed in a better world for all, one where everyone, no matter their background, was treated fairly. My father had seen, first hand, the effects on a child of draconian parenting – his own mum and dad locked him in cupboards for long periods of time as a boy – while my mother was the kind of woman who would cry over a mistreated button (she claims the contents of her mum's sewing box were the only things she was given to play with as a child).

We were probably quite a dysfunctional family, but then what family isn't? And I didn't know anything else. I just thought, mostly, that they were pretty cool, because I was not subject to the same rules and regulations as most of my other friends were. When Katie was having her fingernails painted with foul-tasting varnish to stop her sucking her thumb, my mum said it was inhumane and that if I self-soothed through thumb sucking, then that was absolutely fine. While school friends were denied the latest Hello Kitty set because they had to save up for it with their pocket money, my parents – both now working in reasonably high-powered media jobs that meant we rarely saw them, my mother as a writer at a newspaper, my father in advertising – would come home laden with toys from their various work trips. And while most of my friends had strict curfews as teenagers, it was my house they were having to come home from, after my parents turned our garage into something my friends and I called 'the love shack', a glorified shed at the end of the garden where we could drink and smoke to our heart's content without my parents interrupting us, my parents believing that it was always going to happen, so it may as well happen in plain sight. 'We don't want you keeping secrets from us!' my mother would trill, when she suggested the idea. 'I would rather you were partying safely under my roof than out on the streets where ANYTHING COULD HAPPEN TO YOU!'

If it happened in front of them, how bad could it be? It was sweet, really, how willing they were to put their trust in me. How ready they were to believe that I would never, ever keep anything from them.

I keep thinking about some of the things I did, some of the places I found myself in. The hotel rooms. Endless hotel rooms, with people I would not be able to pick out in a line-up. The stairs I found myself on, my skirt hitched up around my waist, a man standing over me, telling me it was time to get in my cab. The milky stain on my coat one morning, that I could not explain but could guess at. The blood all over my sheets, like a murder scene, after I fell down the stairs of my flat and tore open a cut on my knee, another drinking injury that was just healing over. The pain in my lower back I woke up with most mornings of my twenties, which I put down to sleeping funny when I must have known, deep down, that it was my kidneys trying to process the excess of the night before. The friend who came to visit from Birmingham for the weekend when Edie was only one, the friend I believed would be up for a fun night of drinking in the garden, the friend who the next day told me she was worried about me because I had got drunk pretty quickly and what would have happened if something was wrong with Edie? I never saw that friend again. The hooking up with strangers over the internet. The time I had called a PR, drunk and high as I made my way home from a night out at 8.30 in the morning, to tell them I wasn't well and wouldn't be able to make the interview with their client; and the worried call the PR made to my boss after, telling her she thought I was drunk. The constant lies I told my boss to get myself out of trouble. And so much more I really can't tell you, because for now, this is enough. This will *have* to be enough. Any more, and I might have to drink myself into oblivion to numb the shame.

Shame. How many times will I type that word in this book?

*

There are some people – many people, in fact – who are so ashamed of their drinking that they feel they cannot tell anyone about it. Certainly I have fallen into that category. I have minimised my drinking, laughed it off, taken the events that have happened during my drinking and polished them into amusing anecdotes to retell for others' amusement, as if I were some Gatsbyesque creature and not a tragic mum in her late thirties drinking herself into a stupor in the back garden on her own. I have, at times, been so ashamed of my drinking that I haven't even been able to be honest with *myself* about it, my head trotting out a selection of justifications designed to placate me: you have a stressful job; you are super fun when you drink; life is too short to beat yourself up for indulging in a few pints of lager of an evening; it's not as if you drink spirits; it was sunny today; it was rainy today; it was a day with a Y in it.

But now I know that if I don't tell everyone about it, I will never escape it. I will be stuck in a pathetic cycle, lying to myself and everyone else, until one by one everyone will have given up on me, exhausted by this constant dance of denial. This is where I am heading. This is where silence and secrets and shame will take me: nowhere good.

But if I tell everyone about it, I will take myself to a place where I am held accountable. If I tell everyone about it, I can own what is happening and start to move on. If I tell everyone about it, I am choosing to live in truth, and while choosing to live in truth doesn't always take you to the nicest places – not glitzy bars nor the best parties – it will take you to the *right* places, the places you are supposed to be. Rehab, for example.

So I call my boss and confess everything to her. She sounds relieved, not angry. I call my friend Martha: again, relief. I text the girl I had my last crazy night with, submitting my confession – all my confessions, in fact – and a sort of apology for my behaviour. A tacit acknowledgment that I have fucked up, and that I will now be beginning the process of unfucking things up. 'I'm sorry that this is happening to you,' she replies. My body is a bag of relief that she is no longer ignoring me. 'Thanks for letting me know!' It's as if I've messaged to let her know that I am going to be late for dinner, though frankly, how else do I expect someone to respond?

I find myself gripped by a sort of confessional madness. I put it on Instagram. On Twitter. On Facebook, even. I tell the acquaintances I bump into on the street. 'How are you?' they say. 'Oh, about to go to rehab!' I chirp back, as if I have just announced I am off to Spain for my holidays. I am suddenly appearing in everyone's lives unannounced, to play to them the story of my very own disaster movie. Does it ever occur to me that not everyone needs to know? That people might be dealing with their own issues, that my drama is but one drama taking place in a world stuffed full of them? But in my mind, addled and swollen as it has been by booze, my story is the only one that matters right now, and every time I tell someone, I feel a little more safe; I feel that I am putting some sort of narrative distance between me and the things that have happened to me while under the influence.

Perhaps I should be walking around with a big sign above my head saying 'I AM GOING TO REHAB!' It's not that I'm proud of myself . . . quite the opposite. It's that I can't quite believe that it is happening to me, and by telling people I am making it true. I am going to rehab. I am going to rehab. I am going to fucking rehab. And I know this looks bad, but believe me . . . it feels even worse.

On the Friday before I am due to start rehab, they come. They arrive like sentinels, waiting for the moment I am at my most uncontained, and then, just as I am about to boil over and burn all the surfaces around me, they make their move. In they swoop, one after another, blinding me with their intensity, offering me sweet relief from the voices in my head: the cravings. The cravings for another drink.

They know that I am too long in the tooth now to fall for the old 'just have one' craving. I am more certain than I have ever been about anything in my life that I will never have just one, that I would never *want* just one. That if some scientist were to announce that she had come up with a pill that made its user moderate their drinking, I would not be interested in taking it. That the only pill I want right now is oblivion. So the cravings offer this to me like a gift, exquisitely wrapped in beautiful ribbon: sweet, sweet nirvana, the opportunity to go under one last time.

To start at rehab, I need to have seventy-two hours clean time behind me. This means that, by my estimations, I can have my last drink sometime in the early hours of Saturday morning. Which means, by these same estimations, that tonight is my last opportunity to drink before I must stop forever. Forever! Forever and ever and ever, until the die that I die, I will never be able to answer the clarion call of oblivion. I am never going to drink again, and so now I must drink. I must. What else is there to do?

The day is bright, blue. I take my child to a picnic that has been arranged by her new school: for the day after I start rehab, she will start in reception. This get-together is a chance for parents and their children to get to know each other before starting education together, and it is perhaps testimony to my alcoholism that I spend the entire duration of it planning the binge I am going to have when I put my daughter to bed that night. Indeed, it is a testimony to my alcoholism that my daughter starting school has paled into insignificance against the fact of me starting rehab; that one of the most important days in my child's life could be completely subsumed by my desire for alcohol. That my drinking could take me to a place where it matters more than my own flesh and blood.

Sitting on the common, I try to engage other parents in conversation. But all I can think about is the twelve-step meeting I attended during my thirty-five-day alcohol-free stint, when I heard someone say that they put their drinking ahead of their family. I remember the relief I felt at hearing those words, the tears I sobbed; and now I would do anything to unhear them, to stop them from dancing across the scene unfolding in front of me: parents laughing and smiling together with their children, easing their nervous offspring into friendships with other uneasy four-year-olds.

What does it say, that in maturity terms, at least, I feel I have more in common with these children than their mothers? I don't deserve to be there. I don't have any right to my daughter any more. I am going to rehab, and planning my last drink, while she looks to me for some sort of guidance I feel unable to give her. If I could tell her anything, anything at all, it would be to not turn out like me. To think about what I might do, and then learn pretty quickly to do the opposite. My parents had often told me I was a selfish child, that my moods dictated the mood of the entire family, and now, even as an adult with my own family, I cannot manage to be different. All that matters is me. And my drinking.

I make a good stab at making small talk with some of the parents, as my child plays mermaids with a little girl. I can hear that words are coming out of my mouth – we're so pleased to be in the catchment area; we've heard it's a great school with fantastic pastoral care; apparently they can take Mandarin! – but my head is just a mass of road blockades, each thought eventually coming up against the cravings, and the absolute knowledge that I have to drink. After an hour, I make our excuses and leave, reasoning that I have another six years to spend with these people. I take Edie's hand and we walk along the common, me squeezing her tightly, my heart lightened by the fact I am about to have one more night of drinking.

This is how my brain works: a thought is not just a thought but an absolute command, and as soon as it comes into my head I have to action it or risk broiling my brain alive in its own toxic juices. I have no ability to detach myself from my thoughts, no ability to rationally assess them, or right-size them. As soon as I have the thoughts, the thoughts have me, and the more ridiculous the thought – drink again! – the more power it seems to have over me.

We arrive home. It is 4.30 p.m. and I surmise that it is best if I get Edie to bed early, because she looks tired and is about to start school but mostly because I am about to embark on my last ever night of drinking. Outside it is glorious. We could go to the swings nearby, but instead I put her on the sofa in front of Netflix and go to see what I can make her for tea.

The fridge is almost empty. There is a carton of milk that contains only some dregs, a bottle of ketchup and some mustard; a vacuum-packed trio of beetroots the only thing in the vegetable drawer. A sad-looking Petit Filou long past its sell-by date sits at the back of one shelf, alongside some butter that has cooled to become one with its packet. Usually there would be alcohol in the fridge but Harry removed it all the day I had declared I was getting sober, taking bottles of beer and some cava and putting them in the outside bins. At the time I was relieved to see the back of them. I did not want them in the house a moment longer, their very presence intoxicating me. Intoxicate. Even the word seems poisonous. But now it briefly occurs to me to go and rifle through the bins to get them; I am ashamed to say that the thing that stops me is not remembering that I am making my child's dinner, but instead that the binmen have been that morning.

I look in the freezer. Some loose peas from a long-finished bag have become frozen in the ice. There is a burst bottle of champagne, which has turned one of the compartments a disturbing kind of yellow. I want to weep at its wastefulness. Eventually I find a single fish finger and two potato waffles. In the cupboard I feel disproportionately pleased to see a can of baked beans. It is a meal, and I set about making it, knowing that every step of the way I am getting closer to the weird, twisted redemption I have promised myself. I look at my Fitbit: 4.47 p.m. Dinner will be ready by 5 p.m. Bath at 5.30 p.m. Story at 6 p.m. If all goes well, I could be ordering beer on Deliveroo by 6.20 p.m. and drinking it by 6.35 p.m.

It occurs to me that I should tell Harry about my plan. That it would be impolite for me to let him return home, unaware that I will be having a few in the garden. I pick up my phone. I am desperate, shaking, nervous about how he will take this, but ready to put on one last performance of a lifetime. It has only been a week since the last one. He answers not with a hello but with an 'is everything OK?'

I try to be as breezy as possible. 'It sure is!' I beam. 'Edie and I had a lovely time at the school picnic. All the children and parents seem really nice. I'm so glad

we got her in!' I think, briefly, about the dogged deter-
mination with which I had set about finding a home
in the catchment area of the school, how this, along
with a garden I could drink in that was not overlooked
by judgemental neighbours, were my only real requirements for the house we would make our home. I shake
it away. 'I just wanted to let you know that I think
tonight we should have one last night in the garden
together, seeing as after midnight I won't ever be able
to drink again.'

There is silence on the line.

'Harry? I thought it would be nice to make the last
drink . . . well, nice! So we have happy memories.'

'No, Bryony,' comes his response.

'What?'

'No. I don't think that is a good idea at all. You said
you were getting sober so you should get sober. I don't
think we should be moving the goal posts at this stage.'

I hear the 'we', and am filled with hope. Because it
means he is not completely opposed to making this
decision *with* me. It means he hasn't discounted it
entirely. I persevere. 'Don't you think that we deserve
this last night of happiness, just me and y—'

'No! No, no, NO!' He sounds angry. And now I am
angry, too. Why isn't he being more understanding?
Why can't he see the position he is putting me in?
Why—

'I'm going to hang up now, Bryony.' I know for sure he is angry, because he is calling me my full name instead of my nickname B. 'I am going to hang up, get on with the work you have so often distracted me from with your hangovers and your comedowns and your endless fucking drama, and then I am going to finish my work and come home and know exactly who I am going to be coming home to. Not a drunk. Not someone half cut. Just a woman who said she was going to get sober who IS sober. Goodbye.'

And he is gone.

I give Edie her crappy dinner in front of the telly, and a dessert of some chocolate buttons I found in the cupboard, the perfect way to distract her from the fury I am feeling as I sit in the kitchen texting her father. Once, twice, fifteen times. Each text is angrier, and more deranged, an increasingly vitriolic explanation of why I need a drink. He doesn't reply. His resolve infuriates me even more. Well, I can show him I have resolve too. My finger hovers over the Deliveroo app on my phone. It is 5.45 p.m. and all my plans are out of whack. I need to get my shit together and start putting my daughter to bed, but I am too pumped with fury to leave the kitchen. I throw my phone against a wall, making a strange guttural sound as I watch it bounce off the plaster and onto the cheap lino floor. The screen has splintered. I need a drink. My life depends on it, I think. I sit on the floor with my shattered phone and I howl. If I don't have a drink I will die, I will die, I will die. I am sure of it, here on the floor with my shattered phone and my daughter in the living room eating chocolate buttons and watching *Paw Patrol*.

I weep and I weep and then I feel a hand on my shoulder. I look up. It is Harry, who has not finished his work, but instead rushed home to stop me from doing whatever it was I was planning to do. I scream when I see him, but it is not an angry scream, not a defiant scream. It is a terrified scream, the scream of someone who does not know how she has ended up in this place or how she will get out of it. I realise that my last night out has to be my last memory of drinking. That it has to be dirty, messy, grim. That any nice memories of drinking will create in my mind the possibility that drinking can be nice. When actually for me, while that can very, very occasionally be true, mostly it is not. And if I change the narrative now, if I replace the fetid, awful night where I let my family down with an evening outside the pub drinking with a virtual stranger, apparently with no consequences, the consequences could actually be far, far worse. I might never get off this god-awful lift of doom.

He takes me up to our bed, tucks me in, and tells me it will be all right. That together, we will get through this. Then he gets Edie, who is confused and also scared. We cuddle together. We cuddle and cuddle and cuddle and I know that I am one of the lucky ones. I have a supportive family and friends and a bank loan for almost ten grand that will allow me to go to rehab. I have a way out. I spend the next three days downing Night Nurse to keep me in an almost permanent state of sleep. Anything to get me to rehab in one piece. Anything to continue being one of the lucky ones.

4

I tried to make me go to rehab

The first person I see when I walk through the door to my new life in rehab is a tall woman with a brunette bob in floods of tears. She wears skinny black trousers, a black polo neck, and a look of absolute despair on her face. She sweeps past me, clutching a lighter and a packet of cigarettes in her hand, and exits through the front door, followed by an awkward-looking man whom I take to be her husband. He has the appearance of someone who would rather be anywhere else but here. Then again, here being rehab, everyone does.

I am a 37-year-old mother with a mortgage and a selection of best-selling books under my belt, but I feel about twelve. I am wearing a pair of leggings and a hooded jumper, the hood pulled up over my head as some sort of protection from . . . what, exactly? The reality, that I am an alcoholic an alcoholic an ALCOHOLIC and have failed so badly at life that I have landed myself in rehab? I am trying to remember the last time I felt this scared, this small, this out of my depth, and it must have been my first day of secondary school. I stand awkwardly in the hallway, waiting for someone to notice me, to help me, to *save* me. I want someone to scoop me up and provide me with a set of clear instructions that will lead me to sobriety and salvation. Instead, a man appears out of an office door clutching a small, clear, plastic pot, the type that you are given in doctor's surgeries when they want a urine sample.

'Bryony?' he says, flatly. No smile. Not even eye contact. No bunting or welcome signs *here*.

'Yes that's me!' I trill, as brightly as is possible in the circumstances. Even now, there are layers of denial, remnants of Fun Bryony to which I must cling. He hands me the plastic pot and tells me I need to pee in it. 'We need to check you have no alcohol or drugs in your system before we can allow you to start.' Again, no small talk. No sweet talk. Just the cold, hard stare of a person who does not trust me, a person who has absolutely no reason to trust me. To him, I am just another addict and alcoholic, a human who needs help.

A human who needs to pee in a pot to prove she is not under the influence before she is allowed to receive it. I take the pot and head to the loo. And so begins the first day of my twelve-week stint in rehab.

Having peed in the pot and handed it back to the man in the office, I am told to sit in the waiting area until further notice. I do as I am told, and stare at walls covered in notices about who is on fag-sweeping duty this week. The woman with the brunette bob returns. She has stopped crying, and seems to have lost the husband, but looks exceedingly pissed off. I try to catch her eye and smile but she is not having any of it. She marches through the hall, an icy glare fixed on some room in the distance, into which she disappears, shutting the door firmly behind her. I am not feeling a whole lot of warmth so far, other than from the pot I pissed into, but then what did I expect? To be cuddled and held by accommodating staff bearing waffle robes and expensive herbal tinctures? Whale music, soft lighting, scented candles? The weight of what is happening bears down on me. I begin to panic. What are they doing with my pot of piss? Why is it taking them so long? How dare they ask me for such a thing! Me! A successful, grown woman! I want my pot of piss back! Oh God. What if it has traces of alcohol and drugs in it? What if I have already failed before I have even got started? Goddamn this pot of piss and all who sail in it!

The office door opens. A different man comes out. He looks a little friendlier, and is at least smiling. Also, he is not holding any pots to piss in, just a notebook and some forms. 'You must be Bryony,' he grins widely. I nod back. 'I'm Peter,' he says, putting a hand out to shake. 'For the next twelve weeks, I will be your counsellor. Now, shall we get started?'

'Does this mean I've passed?' I say, hopeful.

'You've passed?' He seems confused.

'The urine test?'

'Oh right, yes, you've passed. Better get used to them, I'm afraid. Right, follow me and we can get this show on the road.'

It's not quite the language I would use, but OK.

Bleakly, I trudge up some stairs behind him, feeling like a schoolgirl following a well-meaning but slightly annoying teacher.

'How are you?' I say, trying to find some conversation.

'I'm fine,' replies Peter, 'but I am far more interested in how YOU are.'

My heart sinks.

He takes me to yet another room, all of them, I am realising, identical, with their nondescript chairs and boxes of tissues. 'Sit down,' he says, motioning to one of the chairs, and again I do as I am told. Indeed, it occurs to me that in the past twenty minutes I have done as I am told more times than I have in the entire previous twenty years. 'So, welcome!' says Peter, brightly, as if he is receiving me into a holiday resort and not a rehabilitation centre. 'Can you tell me a bit about yourself?'

I find that, for the first time in a long time, I cannot. I am lost for words. I have nothing to say – nothing that feels *worth* saying. My thoughts are a jumble inside my head, and I do not have the ability to turn them into anything coherent. I suppose that is his job. But for now, speechless and stunned, I decide that the only way I can tell him about myself is via the medium of sobs. He nods along to my sobs, as if he completely understands them, as if they all make perfect sense. Nod, nod, nod, sob, sob, sob. He passes me a box of tissues, and continues to nod as I sob. Nod, nod, nod, sob, sob, sob. He doesn't say anything. Why isn't he saying anything? Why does he not feel compelled to say something comforting to me? He's just nodding, silently, as I slowly but surely sob my way through his box of tissues.

How much time passes like this? I cannot with any confidence say. Eventually, my sobs begin to turn into sorries. Sob, sorry, sob, sorry, sob, sorry, sob, oh my God I'M SO SORRY. Peter leans forward in his chair. 'I'm so embarrassed,' I say, staring down at the globule of snot in one of my tissues. He doesn't say anything. 'I'm so, so, so sorry.'

'What do you have to be sorry for, Bryony?'

Oh you know, I feel like saying. Just *everything*.

But instead I start sobbing again, and for a moment, I wonder if I will ever stop.

I used to tell myself that if something really bad happened when I was drinking, I would remember it. My memories of the night before might be murky and dark, but if there had been a bad, bad thing it would emerge from that murky darkness, wouldn't it? It would have shocked me into sobriety, surely? I had to believe this. I had to tell myself this, because otherwise, what did I have? Yet most of my memories of an evening would start to fade away after a certain point, so that I was left with only endless, endless uncertainty, a blank page which my obsessive-compulsive mind would colour in with the most shocking and heinous things. Abuse. Violence. Sex with strangers. Sex with people I knew. Advances turned down. Love unrequited. Embarrassing secrets. In the cold light of day, there was no end to the possibilities of my awfulness.

It was a cycle of despair that I could not get out of, no matter how much I wanted to. The thoughts of what I might have done, the colouring-in of the blank spaces left for me by my drinking, were so tormenting that the only thing to do was numb them with more alcohol. I knew that if I drank the thoughts away, the next day they would no longer matter. They would be replaced with different, torturous thoughts, but in between I would have a brief period of respite, several hours where the drinking was the only thing that mattered and I could exist in some sort of twisted version of bliss. It was like creating my very own KFC Tower Burger of shame, one layer of shame after another wedged between a bun of it, a load of shame sauce drizzled into the mix. It was insane. Anyone with even a vague grip on their mental health could see that. But I did not have this, and had not, for some time. Perhaps not ever. And so I looked for ways to reassure myself about the way I lived; for ways to justify it to myself.

The Remembering Theory was one of these ways. I would say it again and again to friends and loved ones, casually, jokingly, as if I was at peace with myself and the way my body seemed to respond to alcohol – as if this was some active choice I had made and not a situation I found myself in under the coercive control of mental illness. 'I have no memory of getting home, but I'm sure if something bad happened I'd have remembered it.' Ha ha ha! This theory served me – or at least it served my alcoholism – well for many years, lulling me into some faint feeling of security that was as flimsy as an unlocked door. Occasionally I would notice that the door was ajar – I would wake up with bruises in strange places, notice there was vomit round the lid of the toilet – but I would quickly close it, telling myself that it was nothing, just a gust of wind or a weird mechanism of the door itself rather than anything sinister. It was curious, how I lived in fear and yet did nothing to protect myself from danger. It is only in hindsight that I can see that I didn't think I was valuable enough to protect, that everything inside me seemed so worthless I was basically seeking to destroy it.

Occasionally, very occasionally, something would happen to blow a huge hole in my Remembering Theory. I recall chatting to a friend on the phone, one of my drinking buddies. I must have been twenty-nine, or maybe thirty. We were reminiscing about a night out we had had a few days before, a night I had assumed was largely uneventful: Friday evening, Soho, lots of wine, bit of coke, probably a minicab home, rest of the weekend spent sleeping it off. We said things like 'I liked when so and so demanded the DJ play S Club 7' and 'it was funny when so-and-so tried to snog so-and-so' and then suddenly he said, 'I can't believe I had to tackle that mugger to the ground when he tried to run off with your handbag.' I thought for a moment that he was joking. He must have been. Because I had no memory of anyone physically grabbing my handbag from me, much less my friend becoming involved in an altercation with said person, and surely this would be the kind of thing that would cut through the darkness of alcoholic blackout like a neutron bomb?

'Err, what?' I was stunned.

'Err, hello?' My friend seemed equally stunned that I appeared to have no memory of this event. 'A man grabbed your bag. I was helping you to a taxi. Me and some other randoms on the street had to grapple it off him.'

'Did that actually happen?'

'Yes, Bryony.'

'For real?'

'For real.'

'Fuck me.'

I carried this knowledge around with me, like a one pound coin at the bottom of a filthy handbag. It was there, but it wasn't always easy to access. I could black out through a mugging. And if I could black out through a mugging, I could probably black out through almost anything.

So I start with that.

An hour later, we have done the basics.

Just the basics. The last night out. The times I had

potentially put my child in danger by drinking until blackout. The man at the fortieth. An assault, Peter calls it, as if I had nothing to do with what happened that evening, as if I wasn't the architect of it. I gasp when he says this word. It's like he's speaking another language. It's like he's taking my life, my booze-filled, drug-filled, chaos-filled life that for so long I have justified as just one of those things, and translating it into reality. Into cold, hard facts that are completely unavoidable.

I try to minimise my behaviour, even in this room. Even in rehab. I try to justify it, to explain it. I am seeking his approval, I realise. I do not want him to judge me, to think I am the terrible person I so clearly and actively am. I feel so out of context. So untidy, so messy, so absolutely unexplainable. I tell him that all of this happened and is true, but that lots of other stuff is true, too. That I am successful. That I have run a marathon. That I love my child with all my heart and that on the nights I don't drink I often sit by her side, watching her sleep. And I do not understand how all of these things can be true at the same time. They do not fit the narrative I have in my head of an alcoholic. People are good or they are bad but there is nothing in between, no room for shades of grey. I am a journalist. My job is to tell stories in a clear and compelling way, and I do not like it when something doesn't have a neat structure to it, a distinctly defined beginning, middle and end. I cannot make sense of this strange situation I find myself in. I know that I have to be here, that this rehab facility is absolutely the best place for me right now. But I have no idea quite how I have got here, how despite all the private education and the privilege I have still ended up in this state.

He nods his head at me. He listens.

Eventually, when I have finished with my burbled confusion, he says: 'It sounds like you have had a really awful time, and I am sorry you have had to go through this.'

'I don't understand,' I say.

'What don't you understand?' he replies.

'Why you are being so kind.'

'Why wouldn't I be kind? You are very, very ill, Bryony. How would you treat someone who was ill?'

'I'm not ill,' I snap. 'I'm just bad.'

'You're not bad, not at all. You're a human who is unwell and we are going to do our best to help you get better.'

This seems unfathomable to me, every last bit of it. That I might not be bad, that I am ill, that I will ever, ever get better or feel anything other than this.

Peter tells me that, at the moment, I am chemically compromised. At the moment, he says, everything feels awful because it is, but also because alcoholism has messed with the GABA receptors in my brain, which can cause anxiety. 'I don't need to tell you that alcohol is a depressant,' he says. 'You know that.' I nod – it is so strange how the factual knowledge of something in your brain does not necessarily make it true in your gut. He tells me that on top of all this, my brain has become used to receiving huge dopamine hits from the alcohol and the drugs, dopamine being a hormone that maintains good mental wellbeing. This means that to feel happy it needs more and more, whereas normal people, or people who drink normally, only need very small amounts of dopamine to feel mentally well. 'If you carry on with sobriety,' he says, 'all of your brain chemistry will begin to return to normal, and you will start to feel happiness at small things, like the song of a bird, or the smile of a child.'

I look at him in despair. I am toxic, and cynical, and I'm not going to lie: that sounds like shit.

Is this all I have to look forward to in life? Birds? Laughter? Nature?

Fuck me, this is going to be hard.

It's funny, now I think about it, how I couldn't see a life beyond rehab. Beyond that day, or perhaps that hour, even. How it felt at the time that my own personal apocalypse had happened, and that from then on I was just going to have to survive, to exist, to keep my head above water. It never for a moment occurred to me that the thing I couldn't currently imagine a life without – alcohol – would eventually become the thing I could not imagine a life *with*. That I was in the process of encountering people and things that I would one day sit across a table from and think to myself, 'For thirty-seven years, thirty-seven whole years, I didn't know you. I had not even the slightest idea that you existed. Astonishing!' Peter, unbeknownst to me, was one of them. And so was the brunette girl with the bob. The one who wouldn't meet my eye. The one who swept past me as if I were furniture. The one I didn't exactly warm to.

She was going to become one of the most important people in my life.

I learn that her name is Holly. That, like me, she is a mum. That, like me, she has a problem with alcohol. That she lives about a mile from me, works in a similar industry to me, and that, as I settle in to rehab, she will mentor me.

I learn all this after Peter ushers the rest of the people in the facility into the room, where they begin removing more nondescript chairs from corners and forming a circle around me. It is just like rehab is in the movies: people sitting in drab rooms, with a central therapist in charge who asks everyone to introduce themselves with their first names and the revelation that they are either an alcoholic or an addict or perhaps, if they are in a really bad way, both. But this, I am afraid, is where the movie analogy ends. For in the movie, the protagonist (that would be me), would stand up, announce their truth, and be emotionally and admiringly received by the other people in the room, who may also be in rehab and experiencing their own problems but who, for the purposes of the movie, are largely irrelevant. In reality, I am but one of fifteen people who have wound up here in dramatic circumstances, only to discover that everyone else is going through their own version of your shit and doesn't particularly have time to applaud or congratulate you for also managing to fuck your life up in a spectacular manner.

Holly, my mentor, looks pissed off. But perhaps I am being unfair to her. In truth, almost everyone looks pissed off, apart from the man who is due to graduate today. He seems ecstatic. Possibly . . . high? But that must just be the knowledge that he is about to leave. Peter asks everyone to give their name, their problem, and how they are feeling. 'Then we will come to you, Bryony,' he smiles in my direction.

Nobody else does.

Or maybe I'm projecting.

Slowly, we wend round the room, people revealing

their first names, their poison, and that they are anxious and angry and relaxed and happy and fearful and every other possible iteration of an emotion there is to be felt. I, meanwhile, am feeling uncomfortable at all these outpourings of feelings. It feels strange, and I begin to panic. I am trapped in a room full of strangers, all of them addicts and alcoholics, being brutally honest about their innermost thoughts, and I realise that there is no turning back. 'Bryony,' says Peter, when the last person has checked in. 'Tell us a bit about yourself . . .'

'Well, um.' I stare at the floor, my face hot and my heart fluttering in my chest. I am aware that everyone must be looking at me, so I try to cough something out of my mouth, something bright and breezy that will establish to the group that I'm good fun, a real character, that they would want to go on a drink and drugs bender with me. That I'm not a total bore. 'I'm a writer,' I start, the cadence in my voice a sing-song, 'a journa—'

'Sorry to cut you off, Bryony,' says Peter. 'But could you start by telling us your name and why you are here, and then maybe a little bit more about you.'

A jolt of humiliation shoots through me. How many times today will I, a mum with a mortgage and a career and an impressive back catalogue of Margaret Atwood books, be made to feel like a small child who has just started at school? I feel my cheeks stinging with shame.

My eyes begin to water. I begin to say sorry, because at the moment apologies feel like the only thing I have to offer the world. 'Sor—'

'You don't have to apologise,' says Peter. 'There's nothing to apologise for here. Just breathe. You are amongst friends here.'

I glance around the room at these strangers. They do not feel like friends to me. They feel like the big kids in sixth form, the cool ones, sitting in judgement of me, the newbie. It doesn't matter that everyone in the room has their own, complicated story to tell, that some of them have only been here a week themselves. They are all different, strikingly so, a cross-section of society I would not have expected to find in rehab. I have made my judgement, and it is that they are judging me. Everyone is judging me. I am a piece of shit the world revolves around.

'OK.' I try to breathe. 'My name is Bryony and I'm . . .' My voice trails off at the enormity of what I am about to say. I stop. I take another deep breath. What the fuck, I think. Here goes nothing. 'My name is Bryony and I'm an alcoholic.' I repeat it, try it on for size. 'I'm an alcoholic and a mum and a journalist and I am so ashamed to be here, so ashamed at what I have done. I am scared and I am terrified and right now I feel like the worst person in the world.' I stop, sniff, and realise both my eyes and nose are streaming.

'So yeah, I think that covers it for now.' I break into a proper sob. Holly hands me a box of tissues and her mouth breaks into a sympathetic smile.

It is done. I am done.

Pretty quickly, it becomes clear to me that my little display is nothing out of the ordinary here. If I am embarrassed, the feeling doesn't last very long. I am flooded with a sort of blessed sense of relief, that I have put it out there, and nobody in the room has even flinched. In fact, did someone actually yawn as I announced that I was an alcoholic? Peter thanks me for being honest, and then invites the rest of the group to share their advice on how to make the most of my time here.

'Remember to be as real as possible when you are sharing,' says someone. 'Nothing you can say can shock anyone here, and we're all in for the same reason, more or less, so know that we get it.'

'Take everyone's numbers, get involved socially,' says another person. 'We have a WhatsApp group we will add you into later, and we always meet for coffee before the sessions start.'

'Don't give up smoking,' says Holly. 'I mean, if you do smoke. Don't try to give it up at the same time as giving up all the other stuff. You will just make it harder on yourself.'

The whole group nods.

'And if you don't smoke, start,' adds another.

'That's not official advice,' laughs Peter.

I learn that I have to go to three twelve-step meetings a week on top of doing rehab, and that if I don't I risk being thrown off the programme. No money refunded, end of. I learn that by week six, it will be expected that I have both a service commitment at one of these meetings (making tea, basically), and that I will be thinking about getting a sponsor. A sponsor, I learn, is someone who has been clean and sober for a long time, who will take you through the twelve steps of the programme. I learn that I must not eat or drink during sessions, as there are people being treated for eating disorders for whom this is triggering behaviour, but also because, as addicts and alcoholics, we can use these actions as ways to distract ourselves from going deeper into our feelings. This seems uncivilised to me – surely water is a basic human right? – but I realise that I am not in any position to challenge the rules. I learn that I will be randomly drink- and drug-tested throughout my time here, and that there are certain foods I should avoid, like seeded bread, because the poppy seeds in it turn up on a test as opium and might make you liable to being expelled from the programme. 'Happened to me,' shrugs one man. 'The irony is,' he smiles, 'heroin wasn't even my thing! It was crystal meth!' Everyone nods, as if this were perfectly normal.

I learn that for the first eight weeks, I will have to come every Saturday morning to do a 'creative therapy session'. Creative therapy could involve art, yoga or chanting. I shudder at the very thought of this. I learn that during the week, we will be split into groups and do group therapy sessions, or 'P&D' sessions. I learn that P&D stands for Powerlessness and Destructiveness, and involves each person recounting a time that their drinking took them to a very dark place, despite having planned to have a fun night. And this, I learn, will be my first session.

My P&D group is made up of me, Holly, and a young woman who cannot be more than twenty, or twenty-one. She wears her long blonde hair over her face and appears to be asleep. I feel faintly maternal towards her, and the feeling reminds me that I can be a mother, that there is something left there inside me. Our group will be taken by Lisa, a sweet-looking woman who is another counsellor at the centre. Like all the people who work here, Lisa is in recovery herself, 'in recovery' being a way of saying that you are a former alcoholic or addict.

It's hard, looking at Peter and Lisa and all the other put-together people who are in charge, to imagine any of them out of it on drink and drugs. Lisa, like Peter, exudes an air of serenity. She is calm and she is contained. She has the perfect air of someone who has her shit together. She is probably my age, too, which somehow makes my humiliation complete. Surely, if you are going to go into rehab, you should do it when you are young and wild and reckless, like blondie over there. Who waits until they have kids and a mortgage to do it?

Lisa begins to explain a bit about the reasons for the P&D sessions. She tells me that most people in the grip of an addiction think they can manage said addiction, that the next time they use things will somehow be different, even if all the evidence shows otherwise. 'It's the first drink or drug that does the damage,' says Lisa. 'As soon as an addict picks up that drink or drug, something happens inside them which means they are unable to stop. It's like an allergy – there's a reaction in the addict's body which means they don't respond to the drink or drug as a so-called "normal" person would.' Here she uses quote marks, to make the point that nobody is really normal, but that the people in this room are perhaps less normal than most.

'Sometimes, very occasionally, an addict or alcoholic might have a night where they do manage to use in a moderate way. They will latch on to this as proof that they don't have a problem.' I think about the one time I only drank two pints, and thought I had cracked it, neglecting to acknowledge that I had only drunk two because I had a stomach bug. 'But more often than not,' continues Lisa, 'the first drink or drug leads to powerlessness over said drink and drug, which in turn leads to destructive behaviours. All of us in this room have, because of our addictions, behaved in a way we would never in a million years have envisaged when we picked up that first drug. These P&D sessions are a chance to vocalise those things, things that we have probably kept to ourselves for a long time because of the shame we feel about them.'

I gulp hard. I do not know if I can do this.

'In this session, I want you to reveal something to the group that you might not have told anyone. I want you to be as honest as possible, and remember that there is absolutely no judgement here. I want you to know that the purpose of this is not to embarrass or humiliate you, but to free you of the darkness that has weighed you down for so long. There is a saying in twelve-step programmes. "You are only as sick as your secrets." Once we get them out in the open, we start on the path to acceptance – of our problem, but crucially, of ourselves.' And then she says something that pierces my armour, something I don't think I will ever forget until my dying day.

'Shame dies when you expose it to the light,' she

announces. 'So take this opportunity to expose it, and leave it behind.'

I gulp again. I *can* do this.

I listen to the stories of my fellow alcoholics and addicts in a sort of wonder. Holly tells her P&D first, and then the blonde girl, who has a tenderness to her that I see she uses her hair to cover. These are safe spaces, and the knowledge that nobody will ever repeat what you have said in them is what makes them safe, so I cannot break that trust. But what I will say is that as I listen to them, I start to unfurl. It is as if I can feel some of the toxicity leave my body. I had always thought I was the worst person in the world, someone who had no right to be a mum. But all along, Holly had been there, one mile away from me, drinking in the same way I had been. This knowledge slips over me like a soothing balm. It doesn't give me comfort to know that she has gone through the shit I have, but it does help to see the possibility that I have been in the grip of an illness that is more common than I had initially thought, and that I might one day be able to forgive myself.

As Holly speaks, she cries, and I find myself crying along with her. At the end I pass her a box of tissues, and Lisa announces it is my turn. I have always thought of myself as an oversharer, a woman who is quite happy to write books about their torturous OCD thoughts, or the time a one-night stand gave me back someone else's knickers. But now I realise how much is buried deep inside me, how much shame I am carrying around, how little of the truly dark stuff I have actually been able to tell. I close my eyes. I will the room and everything around me to disappear. I feel Lisa put her hand on mine. 'You have been brave enough to get yourself to this point,' says Lisa. 'You can be brave now that you are here.' I nod along.

'OK,' I say. 'OK. I'm going to do this.'

'You can start now, Bryony.'

I clear my throat. 'I'm going to start by throwing myself into the deep end,' I say, numbly. 'I'm going to start by telling you about my wedding day.'

It was a beautiful July day in 2013, one of the most glorious of that year so far. I had woken up that morning full of excitement – not because I was getting married, but because I knew for a fact that the day involved dozens of cases of champagne and that, as the bride, I had every excuse to drink them. This was my first thought when I opened my eyes that morning. Not 'I wonder how my husband-to-be is feeling'. Not 'I can't wait to share my special day with loved ones'. Not 'I hope everyone thinks I look beautiful in my dress'. Instead, I woke up thinking of all the possibilities I had to drink.

I woke up with a very rigid plan in place that I would follow to the letter, so that I didn't crash and fall over before the speeches. The service was at 11.30 a.m. at Chelsea Town Hall, just family, followed by lunch at a pub on the River Thames near the reception venue, where my friends would join us for a big party in the early evening. I knew that if I started drinking early, I would be finished early, so I vowed to pace myself – but I also texted a friend of mine who I knew had a fondness for getting on it, and suggested that she might like to get in touch with her drug dealer, so that there would be some cocaine available to straighten me out, *just in case* I needed it. You know, on the rare off-chance. I was sure I would be fine, but it was good to be prepared for every eventuality, right? She responded quickly. 'Well, seeing as you haven't forced us to buy you anything from a ridiculous wedding list, I think I can stretch to a little present for you 😉.'

This, then, was my priority that day: not the flowers, not the food, not the order of service nor the readings I had asked my mum and dad and prospective in-laws to do. No. My priority was to get as much alcohol down my newly married neck as possible without falling over. I should add that at the time, I was a mother to a three-month-old baby, who I had placed in the care of my own mother for the day. We had used some of the wedding money to employ a night nurse, so that my new husband and I could have our first night of married life undisturbed at a posh hotel. Some new mums might have looked forward to the peace and quiet, the deeply cushioned super-king bed and the chance of a much needed lie-in. But I was just thrilled that I had a window to get as out of it as was humanly possible without having to care for a newborn.

I was curiously numb during the ceremony, unlike my immediate family, who all wept with joy that I had found someone decent to take me on. This was the narrative that ran through the day – that ran through my life, it seemed – and I was in no hurry to create a different one for the people around me. I was a party girl who people not-so-quietly despaired of, who had been tamed by the love of a good, decent man. We had a baby, a flat in Clapham and a Bugaboo. It was all going to be OK. I, too, had told myself that it would be, that this desire to drink was nothing more than a normal reaction to the pressures of early mother-hood. Who *didn't* reach for the bottle the moment their little darling had got off to sleep for the night?

I thought back to my hen do, which had taken place a couple of weeks earlier. It was to be a sedate do at a local pub – I insisted that at thirty-two, I was too long in the tooth to be one of those complicated hens who demands an extravagant dinner, a visit to a spa, a session at karaoke, and fifteen different types of party games. The only thing I wanted, I realised, was to go to a pub near my flat and get pissed with my girlfriends, and my girlfriends had happily obliged.

The morning of my hen do, I had an impression of my ten-week-old baby's footprints made at Peter Jones. I remember standing there, thinking, 'I am a mother. I am a grown-up. Tonight my mother is babysitting while my best girlfriends take me out for some drinks. This is a lovely position to be in. So why am I so filled with anxiety?' I was filled with anxiety because that was what the thought of a planned night of drinking did to me. I wanted to drink, but I was also nervous of what would happen when I drank. I had thought that having a baby would cure me of my wild ways, but I appeared to have picked up almost exactly where I had left off, only without the cocaine. When my daughter was two weeks old I had taken her to the pub and wheeled the buggy back drunk – no milk had come into my boobs and I had not put up much of a fight when it had been suggested to me that I switch to formula. It meant I could drink, and I needed a drink, didn't I? To let off steam, to relax, to remember who I was. A mum, yes, but also Bryony. And if I knew I was able to chill every evening with a glass of wine or six, then surely the baby would be chilled, too? It seemed to be playing out that way. While everyone else in my antenatal group had colicky babies who slept fitfully, I had given birth to a dream who slept through the night from five weeks old. Or at least I thought she did. Some nights, of course, I was passed out cold, leaving my strong, sober and capable husband in charge, the one who had found himself fathering not just his newborn daughter but also his wife.

The hen do had been sedate enough – or at least until I decided it shouldn't be sedate, that is. At what stage had that happened? Seven thirty? Eight? Maybe nine. My friends all wore masks with my big goon face on it. We sat around a big oak table in a pub and drank and reminisced, and then one of my mates pulled out her laptop and told me she had something to show me. Onto the screen popped the face of a very famous television presenter, a man my chum happened to be good friends with and whom I had subsequently met on a number of occasions, one of them being her wedding. I remember standing in the road outside the venue while the speeches were going on inside, waiting for my drug dealer to turn up, and the rest of the evening trying it on with said TV presenter, him politely, soberly, trying to bat me away. I cringed at the memory, and tried to laugh as the TV presenter started a hilarious skit that involved him pretending to cry at the fact I was getting married. My friends all squealed with delight. I just wanted to die, or drink another glass of cava. Either would do. I couldn't *believe* that I used to behave like that. How had anyone allowed me to get away with it?

As a soon-to-be married mum, that kind of behaviour was behind me now, of course. Or was it?

Things went downhill from there. I pressed the 'fuck it' button, the one that was seemingly placed over 98 per cent of my brain, meaning it was very easy to locate. The remaining 2 per cent of my brain tried to reason with me, going through the benefits of taking it easy when you are in charge of a ten-week-old baby, but the fuck it part of my brain had reasoned back that I *wasn't* in charge of a ten-week-old baby at that moment, and that this was my hen do, and these moments didn't come round every day. Why *shouldn't* I have some fun?

I piled into the booze, and continued to do so into the early hours of the next day, when I realised that one by one, my fellow hens had peeled off, until it was just me, standing outside my front door clutching a bottle of cava I had managed to buy from an offie that was still open on the way home, and a friend who was trying to tell me she was going to get in a cab back to hers. I tried to dissuade her, promising that I would pay for her taxi if she just came in and had a few more drinks with me. My friend told me it was 2 a.m. Or maybe it was 3 a.m. I can't remember. She said she needed to get back and that I would thank her for this in the morning. She said that we always had the wedding to party. She disappeared into an Uber and I set about the bottle of cava by myself in the living room, my husband-to-be and baby fast asleep across the hall.

I must have passed out there. I came to at 6 a.m., Harry stood over me with the baby in his arms, saying, 'Good night, then?' I laughed, glad that others still seemed to find me amusing even if the only reaction I could muster towards myself was abject horror. 'Go easy on yourself,' Harry reassured me. 'It was your hen do.' But asking me to go easy on myself was like asking the Pope not to be Catholic.

And now, here we were on our wedding day, another perfectly wonderful excuse to get on it presenting itself to me just a couple of weeks later. My family said things like 'you look beautiful' and 'we are so happy you have Harry' but all I heard was 'blah blah blah, yada, yada, yada, when can we get on the champagne?' Don't get me wrong. I was really happy to be marrying Harry, but I was also really happy that marrying Harry allowed everyone to think I was a changed woman, that I was a *respectable* woman. It provided the perfect foil to the reality that, despite having a baby and a husband, I was *exactly the same woman*. The love of a good man had not changed me, and nor had the love of a gorgeous baby. I was still Bryony Gordon, fuck-up extraordinaire. Now I just had a mortgage and childcare responsibilities to fuck up as well. Pregnancy and labour had not, it seemed, done for me what a solid course of therapy and rehab did for other people, but this was too appalling a fact for me to properly accept, and so instead I did what most people in the grips of an addiction tend to do: I buried it deep, under several layers of Teflon-coated denial. The husband and the baby and the mortgage were proof that I didn't need help, not that I did.

The wedding was beautiful, but I'm only really writing that because most weddings are beautiful, and that is what I am supposed to say. In truth, I didn't actually feel anything about it, other than very over-whelmed. In my fantasies – and there had been many during my mad, single decade – I had imagined happy tears, people gazing adoringly at the vision coming down the aisle towards her beloved saviour. But the reality was quite different. It was nice. It was pleasant. But it wasn't outstanding. It was a means to an end, really, a way of making official something that we had already made official thanks to the joint mortgage and the joint baby. There was no doubt in my mind that Harry was my person, that he was perhaps the only person I could bear to be around who could also bear to be around me (and what else is true love, if not this?). I adored him and his dry sense of humour, his passion for fairness and pizza and rugby, with every last bone in my body.

But in truth the wedding only really symbolised how many layers of denial I had managed to put in place to cover the tracks of my alcoholism. I am sure there were a few people there that day who managed to see through those layers, but they were probably alcoholics themselves, and so were too polite or drunk to mention it. There was champagne. We were happy. There was a little bit of cocaine. We were happy (I was happy. Harry didn't know about the cocaine as he didn't take it). But there was more champagne, and there were twinkly fairy lights and a DJ and more champagne and cocaine and oh my goodness I was SO FUCKING HAPPY. I was the happiest I had ever been, I thought, standing in the garden of the reception venue with a glass of champagne in one hand, my husband's fingers in the other, and several lines of cocaine in my bloodstream. Happy, happy, happy, joy, joy, joy.

Eventually, it was midnight, and my dad was telling the story of my mum throwing her wedding ring down a drain in fury, and my mum was calling him something unspeakable, and my brother was arguing with his girlfriend, and Harry and I decided to escape to our posh hotel. I was happy. I had champagne. And cocaine. Oh, and a new husband, who was exceedingly kind and patient and handsome. At the hotel, we found the bar, where we had more champagne, strangers buying us endless glasses because we had just got married and hooray, we were happy! All the booze made me need the loo a lot. Or maybe it was all the cocaine. Who cared! I was so, so happy, and that was all that mattered.

Eventually, the magic combination of booze and cocaine did its work and I realised I was incredibly, incredibly horny. Sex, I found, was where I went when I had used up all the other highs – the highs from the booze, the highs from the coke – and so it was that I dragged my new husband into the lift and up to our suite where I failed at seducing him because . . . well, because he hadn't been taking cocaine, and it was 3 a.m., and he was tired, and just wanted to go to bed. He fell asleep after mumbling some apologies, and I found myself sitting there, on my wedding night, in my luxurious hotel suite, horny and high and with nobody to take my horny highness out on.

It was a disaster. Or was it a masterstroke? Again, it was hard to tell what anything was at this point of proceedings. I knew I had to take matters into my own hands, and that I couldn't risk Harry waking up and finding me taking matters into my own hands, so I went to the bathroom with my phone and the remainder of my cocaine and the minibar bottle of champagne and a packet of fags and I locked the door and decided I was in heaven. Absolute fucking heaven. Nothing could touch me here, in my own private Idaho – nothing except for myself. I poured myself a glass, racked up a line of cocaine on the bathroom shelf, snorted it, and then in the euphoric aftermath I cracked open the window and lit a fag and started scrolling through my phone for porn to watch. I was so high. I was so happy, mostly that no smoke alarms were going off. Result! It was still dark outside, which was good, which was great, which meant I had loads more time to just sit in this bathroom on my wedding night drinking flat champagne and smoking fags and doing coke and watching porn. Yee-hah! This was the life!

I stayed like this for . . . well, for hours, looking for the video on YouPorn that would get me off. Threesomes? Lesbians? Nothing worked. Nothing was good enough. Nothing would ever be good enough. Not even Brad Pitt and Angelina Jolie right here, right now, in this bathroom, with all the champagne and cocaine in the world, would be good enough. Outside it was getting light. I had reached the point of the evening where I had to accept that nothing would save me. Nothing *could* save me. I was unreachable and unsalvageable. I started to cry. I got into bed next to my husband, who was in a deep sleep. I tried to curl into him but he didn't wake up and so I nuzzled into his chest and I wept and I wept and I wept until eventually I fell asleep. No dreams, just the comatose unconsciousness of the toxic. Dreams were for better people than me, for new brides who deserved their happiness.

I tell this to the room. Lisa looks at me sadly. Blondie looks at me sadly. Even Holly looks at me sadly.

Eventually, Lisa breaks the silence.

'And was this how you had dreamt your wedding night would turn out when you were a little girl?'

I think it might be a rhetorical question.

'No,' I say, starting to laugh. 'No. I think it's safe to say it wasn't.'

And out of the corner of my eye, I see that Holly is laughing with me, too.

5

The shock of the fall

It's as if I have fundamentally misunderstood life.

I have woken up and discovered I am in *The Truman Show*.

I am a human who has believed with absolute certainty that the sun rises in the west. And only now, thirty-seven years into this thing we call life, is anybody bothering to tell me I am wrong.

I'm trying to explain it clearly, coherently. But maybe I am not. I am so overwhelmed with this new reality, with *actual* reality as opposed to my screwed-up version of it, that I wonder if I make any sense. If I ever did. I will try again. It's like discovering that you've learnt an entire language wrong, that the reason people have been looking at you strangely is because you've been asking for the direction to the nearest sex shop rather than the train station.

Everything is different, and yet the only thing that seems to have changed is me.

Apparently, not everyone blacks out when they drink. Peter tells me this. He says that there are plenty of people who genuinely have never ever blacked out from drinking in their life.

Never, ever, *ever*.

He tells me that it is not normal to wake up most mornings and be overwhelmed by self-loathing.

That no, not everyone lives in a sort of semi-permanent state of paranoia. That the majority of people have never considered killing themselves after a night of drinking and using. That there are some people who go on occasional benders and just get on with things without spiralling into a terrible existential crisis.

But, he tells me, I am not one of those people. And never, ever will be.

Never, ever, *ever*.

I am discovering, as well, that my reactions are all off. The way I respond to things that happen to me: apparently, they are not normal. Lisa doesn't understand what I find so funny about her question. She doesn't get why I am laughing. 'What's so funny?' she asks me, when I have stopped giggling like a schoolgirl.

'Do you think that ending your wedding day alone, high on coke, watching porn is amusing?'

I am momentarily silenced. 'I mean, I guess one day it will make a funny anecdote in my memoirs.'

'Is that why you did it?' says Lisa, looking even more sad. 'So that you would have a funny anecdote in your memoirs?'

'Well, no. I mean. No. Of course not. I . . . I . . .'

'You?'

'I did it because it's the only thing I know how to do.'

'And is that funny? Because from where I'm sitting, it seems really, really sad. It doesn't make me want to laugh, Bryony. It makes me want to take you in my arms and hold you. It makes me want to care for you.'

I want to turn in on myself, to shape-shift into the chair.

Later, Holly offers me a lift home. 'As your mentor, I should probably make sure you get back safely from your first night at rehab,' she says, as she steps into the car. Inside, she lights a cigarette and passes it to me, before lighting another one for herself and starting the engine. Little do I know, this is a journey we will do many, many times.

'So how long have you been in here for then, o wise mentor?' I smile.

'Me?' She sucks on her fag, winds the window down and exhales. 'I started a week ago.'

'Oh,' I say, slowly realising that this really is a case of the blind leading the blind.

'I am a massive nine days clean and sober,' she says, pulling into the road. 'You?'

'Nine days as well,' I say. 'I had my last drink on 27 August. At about eight in the morning, I think.'

'Well, blow me down!' she beams. 'I'm a whole six hours ahead of you. My last drink was at about two in the morning on 27 August. I will try to impart what I have learnt in those extra six hours, and it is this.' She stops at some traffic lights, inhales deeply, and then blows the smoke out the window again. 'Everything you thought you knew to be true?'

I nod.

'Yeah, well, turns out it isn't.'

In my next session with Peter, he refers to 'the assault'. I am thrown. For a moment, I consider the possibility that he has got me confused with someone else in his care. It takes a while for me to understand what he is talking about. He needs to prompt me, with mentions of a 'friend's fortieth'. He is talking about the time, not that long ago, when I woke up to find a man going down on me. When I finally realise this, I immediately move to correct him. It wasn't an assault, I explain, it was just a . . . thing.

'A thing?'

'I mean, it was my fault.'

Peter considers this for a moment.

'How was it your fault?'

'Because he had been giving me cocaine all night and I had probably been leading him on. You know how people can get on cocaine.'

'Did you tell him you wanted him to perform oral sex with you?'

I can't believe his audacity.

'Well, no. No. I don't remember doing it. I can't imagine I would have done it. But when there is booze and drugs involved, you never know.'

'Bryony, I think it's really important that you begin to understand how serious things have become.'

I am sobbing. Can he not see that I understand?

'I'm really sorry that all of this happened to you,' he says, calmly. 'I want you to know that it wasn't your fault that it happened to you.'

I cover my face with the tissue and my balled-up hands. Eventually, I speak.

'Just stop,' I say. I suddenly feel very angry. 'Please stop. I'm not a fucking victim. You're making it sound like I'm completely blameless and I'm not. I'm just not. When I was on cocaine I would do terrible things. Really terrible things. I would flirt and I would get . . . I would get in a way that married mums shouldn't get. And I would want to watch porn or I would want to masturbate. I probably said something to him about that. I probably asked for it.'

We sit in silence for a bit, as those words reverberate around the room. My nose is pouring, from the tears, and from all the cocaine I put up it almost two weeks ago.

'Did you ask for it?' says Peter.

'No. No I didn't. You know what I mean. I probably gave him the impression I was up for it.'

'You were out of it when it began?'

'Yes, but that's not the point.'

'I think it is, Bryony. I think it is. I think the fact that you are a highly intelligent, bright woman in her late thirties who has got to the stage in her drinking and using where she thinks violating her own moral code is acceptable, even if it wasn't an assault . . . Well, I think that is *exactly* the point.'

What did it matter, in the end? We were splitting hairs, getting caught up in words. I had, for years, been assaulting myself with my drinking and my drugging. And the greatest crimes that I had experienced I had committed on myself.

It's all too much.

I cannot believe I am here.

I am sitting in the basement of a church somewhere in central London. I have a Styrofoam cup containing sludgy instant coffee in my hands. Until two weeks ago, I did not drink coffee. It was probably the natural thing to have when I was hungover, but I always denied myself on account of the fact I didn't want any more toxins in my body. I know. It's too late to laugh now. It's all in the past, done, over. Now I am drinking coffee as if it were water, or wine, even, and chain-smoking too, from dawn to dusk. I feel as if I deserve *something*, even if that something is a cancerous stick that will almost certainly shorten my life. I have no self-respect, I think we have established. These are my treats, now, and I want to get a T-shirt printed up that says: 'I'm in rehab – give me a break!'

Holly is next to me. We have dragged ourselves here, here being a twelve-step meeting, safe in the knowledge that it's probably not for us, that we will find another way to be sober, and that we are just paying lip service to our masters in rehab.

'I don't want to be here,' I sulk.

'Nobody *wants* to be here,' says Holly. 'When they're a kid, nobody says, "When I grow up, I want to be sitting in a damp church hall with a load of strangers announcing that I'm an alcoholic."'

'Actually,' says the man to Holly's right, 'a lot of us do want to be here.' He says this with a placid smile, not a hint of aggression. Just as if we might find it an interesting fact.

'Newcomers?' He looks at us sympathetically. We nod, slightly insulted to be identified so quickly as new members of this tribe we never wanted to join. 'Welcome!' He introduces himself, and reaches to shake our hands. 'I hope that you enjoy the meeting, but if you don't, remember there are plenty more in London you can try. There's something for everyone here.'

I have been to a twelve-step meeting before, of course. But then I was going of my own volition, on a sort of fact-finding mission, to prove I was not like anybody in these rooms. Now I am going because I have to, because if I don't attend at least three a week I risk being chucked off the rehab programme and then I may as well have drunk and snorted the eight grand we have on loan into oblivion. Being told what to do makes me feel furious. I am incensed that I have gone from being an independent 37-year-old woman who could do what the hell I liked to a seven-year-old under supervision and subject to a strict schedule that I must adhere to or risk punishment. I am not an angry person, generally, but right now I feel it multiplying in my body, a toxic miasma spreading to every cell. I am fuelled not just by shame, but self-pity, and I am not sure there could be a worse combination. How come everyone *else* gets to drink alcohol when life is difficult, while I have to sit here in a miserable church hall drinking crap coffee?

Poor me, poor me, pour me another drink.

I could say all of this, of course. I am in a twelve-step meeting. The very point of going to these meetings is that you can say stuff like this. But I don't want to talk. I just want to sit, and sulk, and fume.

In meetings, people share that they are grateful to be alcoholics. They seem happy. They seem kind, considerate, and welcoming. They offer you tea and their phone number, telling you to call if you are struggling with sobriety. They give you hugs. Some of them claim to be many years sober, and that before they got sober they were just as bad as I was, if not worse. But I don't believe them. I can't believe them. And I certainly don't trust them, these nice, kind, genuine-seeming people who want to give me a hug and tell me it's all going to be OK. Are they mad? Do they know what I've done, how I've behaved? When you don't even trust yourself, it's hard to put your faith in anyone else. Still, I tell myself that they are not my people. Except, awfully, that they are. For now at least.

Back at home, after the meeting, I google things like 'why twelve-step meetings are rubbish' and 'why twelve-step meetings don't work' and 'ways to get sober that don't involve twelve-step meeting'. On the last count, not a lot comes up. What was I hoping for? A magic pill that would take away my cravings and hand me back my sanity? I remember, a couple of years ago, my psychiatrist telling me about the twelve-step program, but also about a drug called Antabuse, that worked by making you very ill if you consumed alcohol. I begged her for it, but she refused me, because she said I wasn't there yet; she said it was a very dangerous drug to prescribe, and that she would rather I tried meetings. I scoffed. She didn't know me. But now I saw that she did. She knew me. She saw me. And had I listened to her, I could have been through this years ago.

There is no easy way out of this, I realise, with a jolt. I begin to cry. I throw my already shattered phone on the floor again, though luckily this time it is carpeted. I go into the garden and smoke. I drink more coffee. So much coffee. From none at all to seven cups a day in the blink of an eye. I pace the world angrily. I am an alcoholic. But mostly, I am in shock. Cold, hard, shock.

It wasn't just when I was drunk that I would do terrible things. I would do terrible things when I was sober, too. I had become so used to hangovers that I didn't even know that was what they were – I just thought everyone walked around to a soundtrack that consisted mostly of the low hum of dehydration and occasional nausea.

I did not get the shakes when I stopped drinking. OK, I'd only once got the shakes when I stopped drinking, but that was after a particularly heavy period of Christmas parties, so I immediately dismissed it as just one of those things. Brushing my teeth would often make me retch, but I just assumed that was an early morning thing, rather than an alcohol thing. My stomach was almost permanently upset, but it was never embarrassing, and sometimes I even liked the feeling of everything rushing out of me in the morning – it was as if I was emptying myself of the night before. What I'm trying to say is that my hangovers weren't like other people's hangovers. They weren't epic, and they didn't involve staying in bed for days. I had never had a headache, or so I thought. I seemed to function. I did my work. I showed up. People told me that I had the constitution of an ox, and I took it as a compliment. But I was not an ox. I was a duck, seemingly serene above water but paddling frantically to stay afloat underneath.

Mostly my hangovers showed themselves in my irritability with the people closest to me. My husband. My child, I am and always will be ashamed to say. I would take all the toxins out on them – they got my low moods and my lethargy, while everyone else got to see bright, bouncy Bryony. I thought that their love was unconditional, and that my moods could be excused by this, but I did not seem to realise that you could love someone unconditionally but also not like them.

I remember, when Edie was about eighteen months, taking her out for some lunch to a café near our home. I thought she could do with the fresh air. I thought *I* could do with the fresh air. The café was packed with other mums and their buggies. It was noisy and chaotic, like my hungover head, but I found a spot for us and set about ordering something healthy for us both, featuring lots of broccoli and leaves. The kind of thing that someone might see my daughter eating and think, 'Gosh, what a good mother she must have!'

But my daughter didn't want to eat it. Of course she didn't. She was eighteen months old, and the things she put in her mouth were the only things she had any control over – a bit like me, now I come to think about it, although for very different reasons. I was cranky and hungover half the time and probably didn't give her the required amount of attention, but I had allied myself with the slummy mummy school of parenting and justified my behaviour by telling myself that it was better my daughter had a good, honest, female role model, rather than one who baked and smiled all day long, compliant at all times. Edie threw the broccoli on the floor. I asked her not to. She threw some more on the floor. I started to feel my temper rise. If I could just get some broccoli into her, everything would be OK, and I would win at parenting for the day. Why was she being so difficult?

I tried, softly, to reason with my toddler. She turned her face from me in disgust. My whole body felt the shame of it. I got up, took her out of her high chair, and took her to the disabled toilet, where I knew there was a hand dryer. Edie hated the sound of hand dryers. They made her cry and cover her ears in terror. They shocked her, these innocent-looking boxes on the wall that suddenly screamed and shouted at you if you went anywhere near them. The hangover had removed most of my patience and the broccoli incident had taken the little that remained.

'If you don't eat your broccoli, I will turn the hand dryer on.' Edie hid in the corner. 'Do you understand?' I said, fiercely.

She nodded. She understood as much as an eighteen-month-old could. I unlocked the door, took her back, and repeated my threat. But still she refused to eat the broccoli, throwing it onto the floor alongside the other wasted florets. I marched her back to the disabled toilet, locked the door, and turned the hand dryer on. She began to wail and sob. Shame stung me like a swarm of bees. What was I doing? I took her in my arms and I apologised, again and again and again, willing the hand dryer to turn off. I tried to make it up to her by feeding her a brownie. We spent the rest of the day at home, on the sofa, watching CBeebies as I played Candy Crush on my phone and stroked her hair absentmindedly. That night, I drank the stresses of the day away. I deserved to, didn't I? The day I'd had.

I'm telling you this because I need you to know. I need you to know that this is the madness of alcoholism. That it does not always involve violence and injury and physical harm to yourself or others. That sometimes the harmful effects are less obvious, more creeping and insidious than that. That sometimes they're a series of actions that seem like nothing but mean everything, like putting your baby to bed without a story so you can crack open the wine a bit quicker, or losing your cool when your baby won't eat broccoli.

But also, maybe, I need you to know that you are not alone.

I thought I had escaped most of the awful physical symptoms of hangovers while I was drinking. But now I had stopped, I seemed to be getting them all at once.

In those early days of sobriety, I felt I deserved every last symptom I experienced. Every awful last thing.

I had been told that because I was a binge-pattern alcoholic, I would not have to dry out under medical supervision. (Having thought that you couldn't be an alcoholic if you were a binge drinker, I was now discovering that, on the contrary, a massive 60 per cent of addicts are binge-pattern addicts.) For top-up drinkers – that's people who drink almost all day, every day – it is imperative that they are properly detoxed, as sudden withdrawal from alcohol can actually kill people. Perhaps naïvely, I had assumed that because I didn't fall into that category, I wouldn't have any physical symptoms of detox.

As if it was an either/or situation. As if everything was black or white, and there were no shades of grey in between.

I had not expected to get off scot-free, but nor had I envisaged a scene from *Trainspotting*. I often heard it said that one of the benefits of giving up alcohol was that you started to feel physically much perkier, that your sleep got better and your skin became brighter. But with me, none of this seemed to be happening. In fact, the very opposite was true. In the depths of my alcoholism, I believed it was important to drink through any hint of a cold, as if you stopped, your body would know something was up and suddenly become very ill. Now this seemed to be playing out for me. I had made the first good decision regarding my health for years, and it was thanking me by falling apart.

'The improved sleep and the clear complexion?' said Peter, when I ran through all the ways my body seemed to be rebelling. 'That's what happens when people who drink normally give up alcohol. You didn't drink normally. So of course you're going to be detoxing a bit.'

I was discovering that when you take the constant tinnitus of intoxication away, you start to hear what your body has to say. In my case, it did not sound good. My skin had broken out in a bout of cystic acne, the likes of which I had not seen since I was a teenager. I was confused by this turn of events. Just a few weeks ago, I had frequently fallen into bed without bothering to take my make-up off, and yet my skin was fine. Just fine. Sometimes it even glowed, if only with the perspiration from the alcohol sweats. Now I had given up alcohol and it looked as if it were at war with me. Peter told me it was the toxins coming out of my body, that it would soon be back to normal, but such was the fury of my face, I couldn't believe this would ever be true.

One of my few concessions to good health was avoiding sweet things. This didn't require much effort from me, on account of the fact I generally do not have a sweet tooth. But now, at night, all I wanted to do was eat tubs of ice cream. No, that's not true. All I wanted to do was drink. But I couldn't, and sweet things seemed to be the only way of curbing the cravings, which taunted me from four in the afternoon until eight or nine in the evening, when I would slink off to my bedroom feeling utterly defeated. Again, Peter explained this to me. He could explain *everything* to me. The reason I hadn't had a sweet tooth was because I had been getting all my sugar requirements from the buckets of it you can find in alcohol. Now that had been taken away, my body was desperate for it.

I wondered if the cravings would ever go. Sometimes, I had to remind myself that nobody had ever died from not drinking alcohol, that what I was doing was not going to kill me. Night-time was the worst, the blank space I used to drink in quickly occupied by rose-tinted thoughts of rosé drinking in the garden. I tormented myself with the thought that I would never be able to drink again. I had heard, in twelve-step meetings, that everything was 'just for today', but I raged at this idiotic idea, because it so patently wasn't just for today . . . it was forever and ever and ever, amen, not that I believed in God. And everyone, from Peter to Lisa to the people I met in meetings, kept banging on about Him, or Her, or however I wanted to see the big person in the sky who did not exist. Sometimes this God was referred to as a higher power, for those of us who thought religion was a crock of shit and the reason for every single one of the world's woes. A higher power? A higher power? Perhaps if one existed it might have guided me away from the situation I found myself in now.

I scoffed at this stupid, airy-fairy therapy talk that was suddenly all around me. People spoke of 'boundaries' and 'the universe' and 'feeling the pain'. It made me feel nothing but nauseous. It failed to see the seriousness of the problem I had, of how fucking awful every day was now that I had been forced to give up booze. I believed in nothing, other than the fact I was a terrible person who had fucked up monumentally. I was raging, furious, ready to explode. I told this to Peter. He parroted back to me some annoying recovery jargon. 'The great thing about getting sober is you get your feelings back,' he said. 'And the bad thing about getting sober? It's that you get your feelings back.'

I am sorry to say I told him to fuck off.

I felt sick, almost all of the time. I could not go in cars without having to pull over and throw up. I was exhausted, utterly exhausted, and yet I could not sleep. A few drinks would usually have done the trick; they would, they would, they absolutely would – one of the joys of alcoholic oblivion was having no problem nodding off. Now, I lay awake for hours, staring at the ceiling, my head churning with all the many ways I had made mistakes in the past and all the many ways I would make mistakes in the future. Harry moved to the spare room. He had been able to sleep alongside my alcoholism but my sober insomnia, the tossing and turning and tumultuous sobbing, was a nightmare too far for him.

I realised I was afraid of the dark. I was a grown woman, and I was afraid of the dark. It was stunning, this realisation that I had numbed for so long with alcohol. When the lights went off, I panicked. I came alive with terror. The pressure of having to sleep, of having to hand my body over to the unconscious care of goodness knows what was too much for me. I borrowed one of my daughter's night lights. It was small and yellow and shaped like a star. It plugged into the socket, and gave out a permanent low glow that turned my marital bedroom into the bedroom of my childhood, when my mum had peppered the room with similar lights and given me a set of Mexican worry dolls to sleep with under my pillow. But then I was a child who had every reason to be scared, because isn't childhood terrifying? The not knowing how your life is going to pan out, the fear of abandonment when you lose your mum for even a minute in the super-market. Now I was thirty-seven, and I knew better: I knew how my life had panned out, and that my mum was not going to abandon me in the cold meat aisle. Did this somehow make it worse, that despite all of this I had still managed to abandon *myself*?

I lay awake for hours, trying to fathom how I had messed up so spectacularly. When my body eventually relented and delivered me to something approaching sleep, it began to punish me in other ways. Namely, through the complicated process of trying to repair all the damage I had done to it over the years. It sweated everything out of me, night after night after night, so that sometimes I woke up to the soft glow of the toy light, shivering and so soaked that I had to get up and put a jumper on before changing the sheets. When I woke up in the morning, I felt as if I had gone several rounds in a boxing ring. Everything hurt. Every muscle, every joint, every tissue of my body and my being. I couldn't believe I had done this to myself. Or that I was doing this to myself. Were things ever going to get better? What, exactly, was the point?

This was the point:

Imagine if every morning, you woke up and the first thing that popped into your head was how disappointed you were with yourself. Not 'what a lovely day', not 'I can't wait to get started', but 'oh wow, I have managed to fuck everything up without even moving a single muscle'.

This was what life was like when I was drinking. Almost every day I woke up not to an alarm clock, but to the knowledge that I had broken the promise I made to myself just twenty-four hours earlier. Almost every day I woke up to the knowledge that I had failed, that I had let everyone down again, that there was probably some sort of damage limitation to be done: with my friends, with my husband, with myself. It was a tough place to come back from. I never really gave myself a chance. I was always on the back foot, apologising for my actions, my words, my *existence*. Was it really any surprise, then, that by the time I got to 4 p.m. I was so utterly drained by the effort of living that the most tantalising option open to me seemed to be the sweet taste of oblivion that existed at the bottom of a bottle?

Now, I open my eyes and for a moment, a tiny moment, I am in my default position. Disappointment. Dismay. How can I have done this *again*? Then it dawns on me. It floods me. Relief. Absolute relief. I am safe. I have not been drinking. I am here, in my bed, and my body may ache and I may be exhausted but I am not hungover. I am not hungover. I am not a drinker. I am fifteen days, sixteen days, seventeen days, eighteen days, more, more, *more* . . . and up and up the counter goes, this glorious feeling in the morning perhaps the only thing that stops me from picking up a drink when the cravings arrive in the afternoon.

They are bad, these cravings, but I also know that they are normal. It would be stranger, I tell myself, if they weren't there after all these years of drinking. And they remind me that I have a problem. They are proof not that I must drink, but that I must not. The existence of the cravings is, in itself, evidence that I am doing the right thing by going to rehab. Whether I like it or not, the forced twelve-step meeting attendance and the endless counselling are enabling me to step back from my thoughts and my cravings for the first time in my life, rather than diving straight into them.

And then there is Edie.

Precious, wonderful Edie.

In the morning, once I have enjoyed the feeling of relief, I get up, and I make her breakfast. It is a small thing, an obvious thing, a thing that happens in households around the world every day. Parents on autopilot, getting their kids ready for school. But for me, it is almost miraculous. The whole process feels like a sort of magic. From pouring the milk and cornflakes into a bowl, to the very fact we have milk and cornflakes to put into a bowl. I take my time to brush her hair and her teeth, not rushing as I would have done just weeks ago, when Harry always had to get her ready because I couldn't – or wouldn't – get out of bed. *Just ten more minutes. Just five more minutes. I'm sick. I think I might be coming down with something.* And all the other excuses I used day after day after day to try to stay under the duvet in my own sweat and self-loathing, a place I didn't even want to be but was too terrified to leave for fear of what I would encounter when I did. It was like suffering from Stockholm Syndrome. I knew that the alcohol made me feel this way, but I didn't have the strength to try to escape it. It was all I knew, and there was a sort of safety in that, even when it felt horribly dangerous.

143

Now I had managed to flee the alcohol, for the time being at least, and in the morning, I felt the absolute joy that I imagined recently released hostages did. Almost three weeks after my loathsome last drink, I woke early, feeling bruised and battered but desperate to get up. Desperate to live these hours that had previously been lost to me. It was Saturday. I had creative therapy in a couple of hours, but there was plenty I could do in that time. I went into Edie's room and watched her sleep for a bit. Then I crept downstairs and made myself the first of many coffees. I decided I would go for a run. Half an hour later I returned, breathless and amazed by what I had seen. Harry was coming down the stairs in his dressing gown, wiping sleep out of his eyes. 'Well, this is certainly . . .' He appeared to be lost for words. 'Different?'

'Almost twenty-one days!' I beamed. 'I thought I'd celebrate with a jog. God, it's lovely out there. And you won't believe it. I was hoping I'd see loads of hungover people traipsing home, so I could feel smug. But instead all I saw were other people running! Like, loads of them! Up and out in the park before 7 a.m. on a Saturday! There must be something in the air. You know, I'm so glad that I've decided to get sober at a time when people are suddenly starting to take wellness seriously. It would have been really difficult before.'

Harry stared at me, as if I was stark raving mad. And

maybe I was. 'Bryony?' he said, putting an arm around me. 'You do know that people have always got up and gone for runs on Saturdays? The only thing that's changed is that you've decided to join them.' I didn't really understand what he was saying. In twenty-one long, laborious days, it felt as if the world had altered forever. I wasn't ready to accept the possibility that, actually, it had been like that all along.

6

Why me?

The therapy speak had gone up a notch.

We had exposed much of my shame to the light, and established that the kind of terrible things that happened to me – and were carried out by me – were the kind of terrible things that happened – and were carried out by – almost everybody who developed a dependency on alcohol and drugs. The relief of that was working on me like a balm, and I was starting to see that I was not quite the monster I had previously thought I was. Instead I was, in my mind, only half the monster I had previously thought I was. The expunging of that shame, the scrubbing of it from my body, had begun, and it was powerful. I was realising I didn't have to live coated in shame. That I didn't *want* to live coated in shame.

There was a comfort in knowing that I could leave my shameful past behind, that I could be forgiven for it and cleared of it . . . as long as I didn't pick up a drink. That was the killer caveat, and as hard as it was, it did not seem as hard to me as the alternative: constantly living in remorse and with the fear that I was about to be found out.

I was beginning to see another way of living, a hopeful way of living, and I was willing to do whatever it took to keep it.

'We're going to go deep,' said Peter. 'We're going to go back to your childhood.'

'Oh no,' I said, the wind taken out of my sails. 'I don't think we need to do *that*.'

But he kept trying. As if he knew better. As if he were some sort of *expert*.

'Bryony, today I'd like you to tell me something. I don't want you to think too hard about it. I just want you to give me the first answer that comes into your head.'

Ooh, a quiz. What fun! 'OK,' I say.

'Great,' he says. 'So tell me.' He leans forward in his chair. 'How *old* are you feeling right now?'

'I'm thirty-seven,' I say, worried that he might have lost the plot.

'No, I don't want to know how old you are.' He

leans even further forward. 'I want to know how old you *feel*.'

'Oh right,' I say, nodding my head. 'That's easy. I feel about fifteen, most days.'

'I thought so.'

'Doesn't everyone?'

He shakes his head. 'No, Bryony. No, they don't.'

Oh. There goes another thing I'd better unlearn.

Peter tells me that most people who are alcoholic never really mature emotionally beyond the age at which they started to drink. 'It becomes the way that a person learns to deal with life's stresses and strains,' he explains. 'They never really develop any other coping mechanisms. Perhaps drugs, food, sex, gambling. You know, all the normal addictions. But they don't develop healthy coping mechanisms.'

'Sometimes it is helpful for us to think about our inner child,' he continues. I have got used to all this therapy speak, but that doesn't mean I am in any way down with it. Terms like inner child make me want to vomit like . . . well, a small child. Then there are the other phrases that we hear so often from the counsellors. 'Detach with love and without judgement' being one, 'there's no right or wrong answer' being another, and finally, the dreaded 'safe space'.

But 'inner child' is the worst. I explain, not for the

148

first time, that nothing bad happened to me during my childhood, so we can skip this bit of the therapy and move onto the next. Surely Peter should be grateful that I require less work than the normal alcoholic or addict?

'I have no interest in getting in touch with my inner child,' I say, dismissively.

'Oh, I've got news for you, Bryony,' Peter says, a smile breaking on his face. 'You're already in touch with her. She's here in the room with us and she is making her presence known.'

'She is?'

'Yeah, of course she is! I mean, let's start with the way you've dressed today. This is no criticism, by the way, just an observation. You have dungarees on, and earlier I noticed you were wearing another one of your hooded jumpers. Your trainers are pink. You are wearing your hair in pigtails.'

I get a look on my face that is probably best described as sulky and sullen. Maybe even a bit teenage. I pull my hair loose and shake it out as if to show Peter that I am a proper grown-up.

'Peter,' I say, firmly. 'Of course I am dressing like this. I am not coming here to give a presentation, or a talk. This isn't work. I am here to pour out my heart and soul and I want to be comfortable while I do it. That's all.'

'But you're not pouring out your heart and soul,' he says, equally firmly.

I decide to say nothing. I can play his game. I can refuse to fill the silences.

'Bryony, I am not attacking you,' he says. 'I want to help you. And to do that we are going to have to revisit what it was like for you growing up. In my experience as a counsellor, the issues almost always stem from there.'

'But nothing bad ever happened to me,' I say.

'Let's just talk about it,' he replies, patiently.

Though I knew without a doubt that I needed to be in rehab, I had no idea how it had come to be that I had ended up in rehab. I was a journalist, a person taught to ask why at every turn, like an annoying child wanting to know what made the sky blue. In my mind, it was not possible to simply sit and accept a situation for what it was: I needed to know why it was what it was, and I needed to know in detail. I absolutely had to make sense of things. And yet here I was, experiencing one of the most life-changing events of my existence, and I could not find any reasons for it at all. I was stumped. The evidence of my problem was all around me, in lost days and nights and dignity. But there seemed to be no clear cause of my problem, no tragic back story that explained why I had laid waste to my life in such spectacular fashion.

Instead, there was this: a comfortable upbringing, in a pastel-coloured terrace house, with an Aga and a Labrador and a cat called Mittens. I was so fucking privileged, it was embarrassing. People with far less than me had managed to navigate their way through life without resorting to fucking things up. I had a private education, every toy a child could want, holidays to Spain, Sweden and Cornwall. No abuse. No neglect. No untimely deaths. Nobody ever bullied me, except for the voices in my head. I had no right to be the way I was, absolutely no right.

Peter tried to explain to me that mental illnesses affected everyone, not just people who had experienced trauma. I told him I was a mental health campaigner, and that I knew this. But there is a difference between knowing something and feeling something, and I did not feel it when it came to my own mental health – just other people's. I did not feel it because not feeling it was another way to beat myself up, to destroy my wellbeing as some sort of penance to the world for how I had behaved. Now I was waking up to the fact that this 'not feeling it' was in itself a symptom of a mental illness, a way for me to undermine myself and stop myself from getting the help I really needed. I had to go with it. I had paid eight grand to go with it, after all.

'Tell me about your childhood,' says Peter.

'It was fine, just fine. Nice. We had everything we wanted.'

'Were you a happy child?'

'Yes,' I say. And then I realise that this is not the truth. That I was not a happy child. 'No, I mean. No, I wasn't.'

'OK,' says Peter, softly. 'Why weren't you?'

'It wasn't so much that anything happened to me,' I explained. 'It was more that I was a very frightened child. Mum said that I would worry if I didn't have anything to worry about. And it was true. If I stopped worrying about things, then I was sure something bad would happen. When I was seven I worried about nuclear war. I used to worry about fire, so mum bought me a little bell that I could ring to warn the rest of the house if it was suddenly in flames.'

I laugh at the ridiculousness of the memory. Peter tells me it doesn't sound so funny. I am finding that rehab counsellors don't seem to have much of a sense of humour. 'Anyway,' I say, swiping all of it away dismissively, 'I used to worry that my parents had died in a car crash if they were late home from work. All that normal childhood fear.' Peter stares at me intently. 'And then when I was twelve I got OCD.' I say this as if it were a case of head lice, or a cold.

'Tell me about the OCD,' says Peter.

So I do. I tell him about the obsessive-compulsive disorder that blighted my childhood and much of my adulthood, too. I tell him that I woke up one morning and decided that I was dying of AIDS. I tell him that I saw germs everywhere, that I slept with my tooth-brush under my pillow so I didn't infect my family. I tell him that in time, I couldn't leave the house, and that this went on for a few weeks, and that because nobody talked about mental illness back then, my parents just thought it was a weird adolescent phase.

I tell him that it could have been. That it should have been. That most mental illnesses are treatable if caught early, but that the average time between a child being diagnosed and getting help in this country is ten years. *Ten years*, I shout! But for me it was more like twenty, twenty-five years, because we didn't even know that what I had was a mental illness, that it was OCD. I just thought I was dying. And if you don't know what kind of illness you have, how can you get treatment for it?

I tell him that, in time, my OCD evolved. I started to worry about my family so much that I had to say phrases again and again and again to keep them alive. I would worry that I had said the phrase wrong, so I would just repeat it to myself, in my head, over and over. Then I started to worry that I had murdered someone, or molested a child. I was fifteen, sixteen, seventeen, and there was a voice in my head that told me I was a serial-killing paedophile, that I had done something terrible and blanked it out in shock, and that the police were coming to get me and my life was over.

Eventually, I plucked up the courage to tell my mum I thought something was wrong with me, and she took me to the doctor, and the doctor prescribed me Prozac. I was seventeen. They put me on a waiting list for therapy, but I don't think I ever made it to the top of the waiting list. My mum paid for some private therapy, and in time things started to get better. I did very well in my A-levels. I was high-achieving. I was fine.

Except, I wasn't. My hair fell out, and the doctor could find no reason, other than stress. I went bald. I was eighteen. I wrapped my scalp in head scarves and I started throwing up my food, perhaps as a way to control a body that I seemed to have no control over. One of my first boyfriends told me I was fat, and sometimes he left bruises on me, but he was handsome and could also be charming, and I was desperate to be loved. And then I discovered coke, and it was like I could put a shiny dress on and be the person I had always wanted to be: confident, gregarious, devastatingly attractive now that my appetite had almost gone and I was a bag of blood and bones.

Somehow, I kicked out a career, a successful career,

one that encouraged drinking, celebrated it, and I went from strength to strength. Except, there were always the voices. The voices telling me I was evil. And now I was here, in rehab, proving the voices right.

'And you say nothing bad ever happened to you as a child?' asks Peter.

I answer only in tears.

It is weird, how people can be brought up in exactly the same conditions and turn out completely differently. How some people are just born more sensitive than others. Which is not to say that my siblings are not sensitive – they are – just that they are sensitive in different ways that don't seem to fuck them up. My sister is not an alcoholic. My brother is not an alcoholic. So why am I one?

It was beginning to amaze me, how much weirdness I had made normal, how much dysfunction I had brushed away as being perfectly fine. I had always looked upon my mental health issues as common or garden. Just one of those things. I knew they had caused me great pain, but I did not feel that great pain was anything worth dwelling on, for on paper I had nothing to complain about. I had, in fact, gone to great lengths to make a point of this, writing a book about it, making a life out of it, even. Every bit of campaigning I did was done to make other people feel like this too, to enable them to see their mental illness as an illness like any other, to see their problems as normal, and nothing to be ashamed of, things to deal with and move on from with their head held high. But while I had managed the head held high bit, in public at least, I had not actually dealt with or moved on from any of my own problems. I had ignored them, and set about trying to help other people deal with theirs instead. I was a victim of the very stigma I talked about in public so much. I was so ashamed of my alcoholism that I had pretended it wasn't even there.

But now memories were emerging of times when things were anything but normal, when my alcohol use made my mental illness ten times worse. It was like pouring petrol on a fire, but it was the only way I knew how to silence the terrible thoughts in my head. Of course the thoughts would come back the next day, louder, more amplified, but the next day was the next day, an abstract time that may or may not come, and now was now, and now was awful. So I drank now away. I made now numb, and then I made now disappear. Of course I did. Alcohol was legal and sold in shops. It was a way to unwind. How bad could it be?

I knew, of course, that alcohol was a depressant, that it increased anxiety in the long term. But in the short term, it was remarkably good at masquerading as a relaxant, so good that it could have won an Oscar for its performance. And that pretend bit was all that mattered to me. The moment the performance started to wear off, I would just top up my drink levels and continue with the charade.

I told people that the hangovers made me a bit low, a bit paranoid, but that this was of course to be expected – it was the trade-off for the great fun time I had experienced the night before. What I didn't tell anyone about, what I couldn't even tell myself about, it seemed, were the times when things got a little bit darker than that, when the paranoia became so over-bearing that it started to warp the very fabric of my mind. Sometimes I thought there were people under my bed, or hiding in cupboards. Other times I had to throw out all the bleach and the paracetamol, so unsure was I that I would not try to take my own life. Once, I became so convinced that I had left an iron on that I got a colleague to travel back to my flat with me in my lunch break, so that she could check all the plug sockets. I told myself it was just OCD. Just one of those things.

There was a time when my mother had to take me away. She put me in the car and she drove me to the Dorset coast where she had booked some rooms in a hotel for a couple of days. She could see I was exhausted, that I needed some time with the family. I nodded along mutely. I spent most of the break locked away in my room, convinced that the police were coming to get me, in helicopters, specifically. I would watch the horizon, waiting for them to appear. I didn't know why they were coming to get me, just that they most probably were.

Nobody mentioned the word psychosis. It wasn't for me. I was blonde, mostly bubbly, and I had a successful career. Yes, I had my moments, but with a bit of rest and TLC they passed and I was back to doing what I did best: being a laugh, a show-off, a *character*. Not even when a psychiatrist prescribed me antipsychotics, shortly after *Mad Girl* came out and the utter madness of its success had led me to perhaps *overdo* it, did I see how bad the problem had become. I was struggling again to leave the house. I thought people were coming to get me. But this was just me. This was just the OCD. It was just one of those things, and I would get through it, because what were the other options?

No, but seriously. What were they?

They were this: change your life; stop drinking; go to rehab.

No wonder I had avoided them for so long.

But now I was here, I was beginning to find the place and the people a sort of comfort, a safety net from the big bad world outside. In rehab, I did not have to do normal life. My workplace had given me the time off, and I was turning down most invitations to social events because I had just realised I was an alcoholic and, as kind as the invitations were, the people extending them really didn't need the bother. I had even put an out-of-office message on my email, explaining that I was not out of the office on a holiday but at a rehabilitation course. The noise of the outside world quickly faded away, and people stopped bothering me for things.

The humans with whom I was incarcerated were the only ones I had any inclination to spend time with, outside of my immediate family, of course. My fellow alcoholics and addicts understood and there was no need to explain. There was no need to explain because they got it – they were here for the same reasons, too. It was hard to believe that this motley, multi-faceted crew had seemed so intimidating just a few weeks ago, that they had not been part of my life before. Pretty soon I was welcoming in newcomers as if I had been there for years, and was even given my own addict to mentor. This small act of helping someone a few weeks behind me showed me the progress I had made, even if it was tiny. It didn't matter. It was there, and I was moving further away from the ground zero of my rock bottom.

Alcohol had been my life before, but now it was rehab. I applied myself to it in the same way most addicts apply themselves to things: passionately and absolutely. Every day, we would traipse off to twelve-step meetings together, holding each other's hands through the apparent awfulness of it. We drank endless cups of coffee together, and walked for hours round London, trying to find things that didn't involve drinking, cultured things we had heard about but which had remained invisible to us until now. Between us we could cover every part of London with a tale of drunken, high disgrace, and a great deal of the rest of the country, too. But it was hard for us to tell any stories that did not involve drinking or drugs, and we had been encouraged to explore together all the myriad possibilities that life had to offer outside these narrow fields of vision.

Suggestions were made to us by the counsellors for fun things to do together in our spare time. We could do go-karting. We could play table tennis. We could go to the theatre, or paint pottery together. Just the very mention of these things stupefied me with boredom. These were things dull people did, I had always told myself, dull people being the kind of balanced, healthy people who weren't alcoholics. But it was part of our rehab contracts that we would all go on an outing together every few weeks, and so it was that we would traipse off to some ping-pong club, or a pottery studio, or a go-karting course.

We had to do strange classes on a Saturday morning. These involved painting pictures, and weird mindful activities, and staring into each other's eyes for long periods of time without looking away. On the last count, I struggled. It was excruciating to hold eye contact with someone. Almost physically painful. I wanted to shut my eyes to try to stop it from happening, like a toddler playing hide and seek. If I just closed my eyes, nobody could see me. But I was not a toddler: I was a grown woman, and this was not a game. It was very, very serious. So I stared into my rehab partner's eyes, and all I could do was cry. I had always thought I was a people person, but now I was wondering if, like so many other things, this was actually not true.

The chanting class was similarly mortifying. We sat in a circle as a woman started making strange sounds, similar to a small animal being murdered, which she urged us to repeat. I could stand up on a stage and talk to hundreds of people about the torturous obsessive-compulsive thoughts that made me think I was a serial-killing paedophile, but I could not do this. I could not and would not howl into the wind on tap. One day we had to lie down on a giant piece of paper and let someone draw an outline around our bodies with a marker. Then we had an hour to fill in said outline, in a way that represented how we were feeling. As I painted my body with glitter, purely because it looked nice, I wondered if I was taking part in an elaborate con. But nothing was as it seemed on the surface in rehab. There was a deeper reason for everything. I was told that the glitter perhaps showed a person who was keen to hide their true self behind a sparkly front. 'That's way too obvious,' I laughed, secretly annoyed that I *was* so obvious.

All of these things were designed to take us out of our comfort zone, to break down the endless barriers we had taken great care to erect over many years. Irritatingly, it worked. I had come in here sure I was the very worst person in the world, and now I was realising I was just another person who had taken several very wrong turns. I was not unique. I was not any more complicated than the average alcohol-dependent human being. I was just . . . well, an alcohol-dependent human being. Depending on my mood – and it was up and down like a yo-yo at that point in time – this was either a huge relief or a massive insult.

These wild contradictions were not lost on us. How could they be? We needed them almost as much as we had recently needed drugs and alcohol, the laughs they provided an absolute must when you were spending so many hours exposing your shame. The group sessions were often far, far harder than the one-on-ones, involving as they did hours of sharing, and oceans of tears. It was in these groups that we were all learning boundaries, those far-off misty things that had for so long eluded us. We had to let other people speak, and we had to let other people cry. We had to listen without judgement, without comforting our new friends. We were able to identify what had resonated with us, but we were not allowed to provide any advice, or solutions. The counsellors were clear: the talking and the crying and the enduring everyone else's silence were the solutions in themselves. That was the deal and, if we didn't like it, we were very welcome to leave.

Again it felt like being back at school, when someone would be called on to explain something that had happened in the playground, and everyone else in the class was made to sit in uncomfortable silence, wondering when the stuttering, snivelling explanation would finally end and we would all be free to talk about something else, like the weather. This discomfort, and being made to endure it, was also part of the solution that rehab was providing us with. We were, for the first time in our lives, having to sit with our feelings without reaching for something to dampen them down.

We were living life by someone else's rules, in many cases for the first time in decades, for the first time since leaving secondary education. We had shown quite clearly – by way of ending up in rehab – that our way of doing things had not worked. So now we had to try to do things differently, and live by another book. Unsurprisingly, this did not sit well with everyone. In fact, it did not sit well with *anyone*, but some had more trouble dealing with it than others. Occasionally, someone would disappear from the group, and a counsellor would explain that due to suspension, they would not be back at rehab until further notice. We knew what this meant: it meant they had relapsed.

At first, this felt shocking. It felt upsetting, that someone would just disappear, and there was nothing we could do to get them back. Then it felt like a good way to distract ourselves from our own fucked-up behaviour. And then, awfully, it felt like a relief. It was a relief, because the odds are not great on long-term sobriety, and the more people who relapsed who weren't you, the better. Is that terrible? It is. But it was no more terrible than neglecting your child or lying to your husband or becoming an alcoholic or a drug addict. And there was a power, in itself, in being able to admit to these thoughts, to strip away the layers and the masks and be properly, brutally honest without anyone forming a judgement of you.

Sometimes people clashed. Ever the people pleaser, I made sure I was never one of these people. Some people were good with confrontation, but I was not one of them. It could send me into a spin for days. If someone didn't reply to a text, I could fill that silence with the hatred they felt for me, even if their silence was only filled with the busyness of their own life. I was beginning to see that this inability to deal with difficulties was not normal, that a stern word from someone who was laying down a boundary was not a reason to hit the booze and scramble around for a gram of coke. Not everything was personal. Almost everything *wasn't*. And the person who hated me the most, I was realising, was myself.

We celebrated recovery milestones. Twenty days, thirty, forty, fifty, sixty, in some cases, an impressive ninety. They were all we had to cling onto, aside from each other. How incredible it was that we were doing this, that we were waking up each day and not at any point picking up a drink. To some people, in the outside world, this might have seemed inconsequential. To us, every day of sobriety was cause for as much celebration as a landmark birthday.

Laughter was not thin on the ground. Bemoaning the absurdities of sobriety was essential when you knew that later, you'd be talking about the time you'd woken up in an unknown place with no clothes on. One man was particularly amusing. He was in his twenties, and struggling to comprehend how he would ever date without the aid of alcohol. 'Do you remember the game "Would you rather?"?' he mentions one day, as we walk around the Victoria and Albert Museum in a disinterested haze. 'Would you rather live without cheese or chocolate? Would you rather live without sex or wine? I had no idea I would have to give up both.'

And then there was Holly.

Holly had quickly become my sobriety sister and, more importantly, my soul sister. We had introduced our children to one another, and our long-suffering husbands, too. It was almost as if we had been placed in rehab especially for one another, as if all of our screw-ups and suffering existed precisely to lead to this moment when we would meet. There was nothing we could say to each other that would shock or surprise. There was nothing we wouldn't do to help each other when the other person was in despair – and on any given day, it was usually one of us, sobbing over cravings or our guilt at being alcoholic mothers. I wondered where she had been all my life. Down the road, getting as out of it as I was, it turned out. But it was probably a good thing that we had not met and gone on the lash together. Sharing our stories, I realised that there was an exceedingly high likelihood that we would have gone AWOL and ended up dead.

I didn't have a clue what I was doing, or where I was going, but with Holly by my side I could at least be reminded of the fact that none of us did, not really. Plus, neither of us were in any hurry to lose our shared sobriety date. 'If I relapse, you are relapsing with me,' she laughed, one day. Don't even joke, I thought. Don't even joke.

Early on in rehab, I am told that I have won an award. It is the Making a Difference award, a sort of lifetime achievement award for changing perceptions around mental illness, and it will be given to me by the mental health charity Mind at a big do in a couple of weeks' time.

I read the email from the charity's chief executive, and I start to cry. I feel like a fraud. It doesn't yet occur to me that perhaps the reason I am finally dealing with my alcoholism is because I was so honest about my OCD in the first place. It just feels so wrong, so out of kilter with the real picture. How can a woman who is not even sixty days sober be given an award for changing attitudes about mental illness? Especially when she has been in such denial about her own?

The event takes place in a big cinema in Leicester Square, the kind that usually hosts film premieres. There are a smattering of celebrities, and Prince Harry is there. I take my seat and try to ignore the mini bottles of prosecco that people are drinking through straws. I remind myself I never liked prosecco, anyway. The night goes on, and I realise that my award is the last to be announced. Knots form in my stomach. I feel suddenly very cold, and begin to shiver. Stephen Fry takes to the stage. A montage starts playing on the screen – pictures of me with Prince Harry after we had done our podcast, pictures of me running the London Marathon for Heads Together, pictures of me on one of the Mental Health Mates walks I founded eighteen months ago, that were now taking place nationwide. It is one of those moments you dream about, and as I step onto the stage to receive my award from Fry, I cannot work out why I am not more emotional. I look out at the audience, a thousand strong, who are all beaming at me and clapping, and I am sure that they can see right through me, for I am transparent, nothing. I am just a body, who has somehow done some things. I make a speech, but afterwards I cannot remember what I say. Everything feels like it has been predicated on a lie and, worst of all, a lie I told to myself. I am being held up as some sort of role model, an inspiration, but I have no idea who I am. Absolutely no idea. 'Who am I?', I want to say to Peter. 'Who am I?', I want to scream into the void. But there is no answer. Just a blank space I am going to need to fill on my own.

*

The next day, it is back to rehab. Holly and Peter congratulate me, but otherwise it is business as usual. Or business as unusual, as I prefer to say. Everyone is in their own heads, and rightly so. I am not the most important person in the room, and rightly so. All our egos must be left at the door here, and rightly so. My award doesn't matter here. And rightly so.

I look around the room at my fellow inmates. We are all different, and yet . . . well, there is always an 'and yet', isn't there? So here it is: and yet, we are all, essentially, the same. We have one huge, overarching thing in common.

For whatever reason, none of us have a fucking clue how to deal with life.

7

Why not?

I was being driven sane.

It was quite peculiar. It was wild. It was a form of madness in itself.

One minute I was howling at the sky like a wolf during a full moon, the next I was lying motionless in my bed, too exhausted by my tears to do anything other than sleep.

All the feelings I had numbed with alcohol were making themselves known after many, many years of being trapped inside and ignored. And they were furious. They were deranged. They had been living in the dark for their entire lives, and now the door had been opened and the light was flooding in, they didn't have a clue what to do with themselves. These wild emotions had decades of pent-up energy in them that they needed to get rid of. They sped through my brain and my body, gobbling up the life they had been deprived of for so long. The erratic mood swings reminded me of being a hormonal, prepubescent adolescent, or pregnant.

And talking of hormones, the PMS was insane. In my drinking days, I had proudly announced that I didn't get PMS, but now I was seeing that this wasn't true. I'd had PMS all right – I'd just not been able to distinguish it from the constant cycle of intoxication and low-level hangover I had made my existence. Now there was a fury in me that I did not like and I did not enjoy and that I wanted gone. If this was sober living, then I was not sure I wanted any part of it. No wonder alcohol had always seemed like such a good idea.

I was frightened. I was on the edge. Peter told me that this was normal, but it didn't feel very normal to me. He said that no human can ignore their feelings forever – or that they could, but they wouldn't find it a terribly interesting or pleasurable life. Now I was only experiencing the feelings I had tried, unsuccessfully, to get rid of. They were rearing up and reminding me that they existed, and that they were perfectly valid and had a right to exist. And it was no good, continuing to try to kidnap those feelings and lock them away in the basement of my brain. Feelings and

171

emotions were not going to hurt me. They were not out to get me. In fact, they were often giving me valuable clues as to my state of mind and how I should live my life accordingly, to keep me safe. It was better to just sit with them and get through them, than to try to numb them with drugs and alcohol. The reward was on the other side, said Peter. The reward was life, and all its glorious ups and downs and tedious in-betweens.

But there were some days when all I could do was hide under my duvet, the seconds and minutes and hours of my sobriety ticking up not because I was putting any effort in, but simply because I did not have the energy or the inclination to leave the bedroom or the house. I could manage the school run, where I tried not to let the shame of the situation overcome me for the sake of my daughter. It was not about me, the school run – it was about her. But I could not ignore the paranoid sense that everyone knew my shameful secret, from the smiling, sweet reception teacher who was barely an adult herself, to the other parents who, at my most paranoid points, I imagined calling social services. I knew that was what would await me if I relapsed. I knew that too much was out of the bag now for me to ever, ever go back. And sometimes, when the tornado of feelings and emotions swirled around me, that was the only thing that kept me from checking out.

I had made a tentative friendship with another school

mum, whose son Edie got along with. She was a doctor, pregnant with her third child, her other son born with a genetic disorder that meant a lifetime of special care. She was amazing, and I felt ashamed by how trivial my problems were in comparison. I felt as if my alcoholism was little more than an excuse for self-indulgent bad behaviour. I had been born into nothing but privilege, able-bodied and with a life full of opportunities, and yet somehow I had managed to squander this by getting addicted to alcohol. The shame and the self-pity of it swirled around me every time I said goodbye to her at the school gates and returned to my bed to do nothing other than scream and sob.

There were lows, and there were highs, but there did not seem to be anything in between. It felt a little like drinking and using, when things were either great or terrible, only now all of these highs and lows were taking place in high definition and Dolby Surround Sound, and it was hurting my eyes and my ears and my brain. I would count down the hours until I met Holly and the others for coffee before rehab, but eventually that became too torturous, too difficult, too much like playing a game of Russian roulette, and I realised what I had to do. I had to go to twelve-step meetings. Though it pained me to say it, they were the only place outside of rehab where I felt safe.

*

The first rule of twelve-step meetings is that you don't talk about twelve-step meetings. Actually, it's the fifth, but let's not split hairs over this. The guiding principle of the twelve-step program is anonymity, to protect all those who share in the rooms, but also to remind the people inside them that no one person is better than any other, and that no matter what we do or where we come from, we are all the same: we are alcoholics.

But it is impossible to talk about getting sober without also talking about the twelve-step program. And into the vacuum of mystery that surrounds this organisation, all sorts of misconceptions and misunderstandings appear, misconceptions and misunderstandings that had, for too long, kept me away. I thought it was a sort of cult. I thought that it was religious. I thought I was going to have to say Hail Marys, and renounce all my sins. And faced with that, I thought I would stick with them instead.

Like most people in early recovery, I had a love-hate relationship with the twelve-step program. And actually, maybe it was more of a hate-hate relationship. I hated the clapping, the smiling, the hugging, the holding hands, the people who claimed to be saved, as if I were sitting in some evangelical Christian camp. I hated the happiness, the sadness, the everythingness on display in these rooms. I hated the stale biscuits and the crap coffee. I hated the fact that we newcomers were supposed to announce ourselves as such, and that afterwards people would swarm round you like flies on shit, offering up congratulations and kindness and help, as if this was in any way a normal thing to do. I was used to being hard and cynical and toxic, and I could not understand the openness and compassion. I didn't trust it. I didn't trust anything, other than the fact I was a dickhead for winding up here.

I hated the fact that we newcomers were encouraged to volunteer for 'service' positions, such as making the tea and greeting people at the door. We were told that this was because service kept you sober – the act of doing something for someone else took you out of your own head, and your own head was a bad place to be in early recovery. But such was my toxicity and my suspicion that I couldn't help but think of the fag system at boarding school, where the new kids are used by the older ones as lackeys as some sort of rite of passage or initiation. Still, I did what I was told because I was a people pleaser, and even if I didn't understand these people I wanted them to like me, to accept me, to tell me I was doing really well, that I was the best at recovery, a shining example to everyone else. It was pathetic how needy I was for reassurance, and yet also how entirely dismissive of it I was.

I didn't want to make tea, let alone for a bunch of alcoholics and addicts who were very specific about the way they took it. But I did it. I stood there, in the kitchen of a church, washing up mugs and apologising that there was not any skinny milk or soya milk, as if these people had somehow expected Starbucks and not some skivvy in her first days of sobriety. But I was starting to build friendships in that kitchen, in that church, and I was starting to see that everyone felt this way at first.

I hated the serenity prayer, and the copious use of the word God. I also hated the word alcoholic, on account of how very *serious* it sounded. Then again, it was serious, this situation I had found myself in, and as time wore on and the options for salvation outside of the twelve-step program got slimmer and slimmer, I realised I only really had two choices: die on a hill over words like 'alcoholic' and 'God', or accept them for what they were – just words – and live.

Besides, I was discovering that the twelve-step program wasn't in the slightest bit religious, despite that God word. Peter told me that the twelve-step program worked for people who didn't believe in God, and it worked for people who did believe in God, but that the only people it didn't work for were the people who believed they *were* God. God could stand for Group of Drunks if I wanted it to. It could stand for Group of Dicks for all he cared, as long as I showed up and did what was suggested of me. I liked that, but I could not quite bring my cynical self to get on board with all the talk of spiritual awakenings that was done in the rooms, of miracles and higher powers and moments of feeling utterly at one with the universe. It seemed completely daft to me, self-help talk that meant nothing at all. Was an angel going to descend on me from a shaft of white light and give me all the answers? No. But Peter was always there to explain things like spiritual awakenings in rational terms that made sense to me. 'It's just about getting you to find some humility,' he said. 'It's about accepting that your way of doing things is not always the right way, that there might be another way of doing things, and that there is something bigger and more important than you out there.'

Something more important than me? I was the worst woman in the world, or at least one of them anyway. But I knew I didn't have to believe in God to believe that there was something bigger at play in the world and indeed the universe, that in the grand scheme of things I was but a tiny dot. I only had to think about big bangs and black holes and stars and planets and the fact that the earth only supports life because it is exactly the right distance from the sun to realise that, probably, everything was exactly as it should be, even little old me in a church hall making tea for alcoholics and addicts. There was a comfort to that. The earth's magnetic field was doing its job in supporting life, and all I had to do was show up at meetings and not pick up an alcoholic drink. It was not more complicated than that. It wasn't much to ask, really, was it?

Of course, this sense of acceptance was often as fleeting and erratic as my mood, being run as it was by those pesky feelings I had bottled up for so long. The endless talking about myself with Peter was exhausting. We were trying to find patterns from my childhood that would explain why I behaved as I did in adulthood. It was like doing some of the world's hardest maths equations, and I was the answer we had to get to. My inner child seemed to be getting louder and louder and more infantile, throwing her toys out of the pram left, right and centre. Some Fridays, when it got to around 5 p.m. and I thought of everyone finishing work and getting ready to go to the pub, I could not imagine a time when I would ever be at peace.

It was like a bereavement, and if that sounds melodramatic and ridiculous . . . well, I *was* melodramatic and ridiculous. I was an alcoholic in the very early stages of realising she was an alcoholic. An alcoholic. Would there ever be a time when I would get used to saying that word? Would it ever not feel strange rolling around on my tongue, like some witchetty grub I was being forced to swallow but couldn't? Giving up alcohol *was* like a bereavement, complete with all the steps a grieving person was said to go through when they lost someone they loved: denial, anger, bargaining, depression, acceptance. I could, in my saner moments, plot these out and see them. The denial that I was an alcoholic; the anger that I was being made to make tea; the bargaining that I would only ever have one if I was just allowed another moment with alcohol again; the depression that this would never, ever happen, that I would never be able to stop at one; the acceptance that I was an alcoholic and could not drink again. But the cycle seemed to run and run, and every time I thought I had got to the acceptance bit, that it was here to stay for good, the whole damn thing would begin again, and I would be back where I started, feeling shocked and furious that I had to sit in a room and say that my name was Bryony, and I was an alcoholic.

At home, once Edie was asleep, I took my frustrations out on Harry. Occasionally I would take them out on my mum, who would come and stay one night a week to help look after Edie when I was at rehab. One night I came home and found them sitting on the sofa, watching TV and enjoying a glass of red wine. I couldn't believe it. I was absolutely apoplectic. How dare they drink, in my house, even though it was only a matter of months ago that I had done the same? Harry quickly took the glasses and the remainder of the bottle and poured them down the sink, but the smell was in my nostrils, the tart aroma of the wine coursing through my system. I fell to the floor and sobbed, and then I went upstairs and I threw up. My mum apologised, and said that she thought I wouldn't mind because I never drank red wine. That wasn't the point, I told her. The point was this: I was never going to be able to sit in front of the TV with a glass of red wine, even if I wanted to.

That night, behind closed doors, I raged at Harry. I was always raging at Harry, it seemed. I could not understand why he stayed with me, why he hadn't left. It was as if his patient presence only served to highlight my own awfulness. I wasn't sure, if the tables were turned, that I would have been able to provide the same support, and the horror of that frequently swept through me. The fact was, I had put him through hell, and even though I was getting sober, I was continuing to put him through hell. There were moments when things were good, when things were great, usually in the morning when I would wake up and announce with a sense of relief that I was another day sober, and I would feel a sense of pride that I was able to get up with my daughter and get her ready for school, like any normal mother. But these moments were not in any way a match for the moments when I was cross and weeping and mad, and taking all of this cross, weeping madness out on him.

I felt that I deserved some sort of punishment, on top of the way I was feeling. I felt that him leaving me would probably be an appropriately deserving punishment, one that fitted the crime I had committed. Some nights, I would remind him of the things I had done, of the situations I had found myself in, as if trying to goad him to go. But he wouldn't. He didn't want to. He was steadfast about this and perhaps, Peter suggested to me, getting something from me that he actually liked – maybe, Peter said, I wasn't as bad as I thought I was. Except at home, as the hour approached midnight, I was exactly as bad as I thought I was, if not worse. It was as if I got madder and madder as the day wore on, my sanity leaching out with every deranged conscious thought that came into my head.

Addiction does not just affect the addict themselves, but everyone who, against their better judgement, loves the addict. I knew this, and I knew that I had caused harm to the people around me. I would have done anything to take it back, but at that point in time my head was still too much of a mess that I had yet to untangle. I would perhaps never untangle it. It was impossible to make amends to Harry when I was still in the process of making amends to myself. This senti- ment – that nobody can properly love you until you learn to love yourself – had annoyed me in my single days. But now I was starting to understand the reasoning behind it. Yes, people loved me, even though I did not seem to love myself. But until I felt worthy enough to receive that love, it was basically useless.

Harry kept telling me to *go easy* on myself. To be *kind* to myself. I thought these were annoying greetings card platitudes. It was easy for Harry to go easy on himself given that he had tolerated me all this time and deserved some sort of medal for his endeavours, but if you had frequently got so out of your skull that you put your child's welfare at risk, not to mention your own, would *you* find it acceptable to go easy on yourself? Kindness was something I extended to others, but I was not ready to extend it to myself. I deserved a hard time. I deserved everything I got. It was not fair that I got out of this scot-free, without some sort of clapped-out organ or self-inflicted illness. That I escaped it without even so much as a police caution. I told this to Peter. He responded that if I felt that strongly about personal justice, I was entirely welcome to go back out and drink myself into a far worse catastrophe than the one I found myself in now. I could pick up a drink and I could lose everything, if that's what I felt I deserved. There were sober people who had lost everything – marriages, homes, children they had killed while drink-driving. If I wanted to get to that point, said Peter, I was very welcome to. Or I could stick where I was now, and be relieved that it had never got that bad.

'Because it could get that bad,' said Peter. 'It could and it absolutely would. And then you'd come back here – if you were lucky enough to *get* back here, if you didn't die – and you'd ask me why you didn't get off the train when you had the chance, before it got to the stage it did. And I'd say, "Well, Bryony, you were given the chance. You had the chance. But you decided to throw the chance away because you didn't think you deserved the chance. You thought you needed scars on your liver and your skin and a hole in your heart from losing your family." And you would look at me and see how mad that was. How you could have avoided all that pain, if only you had listened to me and realised that actually, you did deserve the chance. You did, as did your daughter, and your husband, and all the other people who rely on you. All you had to do was stop beating yourself up. All you had to do was accept that you deserved love, not punishment.'

I come home from rehab and before I put the key in the door, I take a deep breath. Tonight I am not going to be deranged. Tonight I am just going to give my husband a hug, and go to bed. I will receive love and I will give it, too.

I open the door and I call his name. There is no response. I can hear the TV on in the living room, but it is not loud, and surely he heard the key in the door?

I start to feel a rage bubbling inside me. How quickly my resolutions crumble beneath me, still. I hear footsteps and then see my husband emerge into the hall, but it is too late. I am furious that he wasn't greeting me at the door with . . . what, exactly? Diamonds, flowers, chocolates? I throw my bag down in the hall, kick off my trainers, and storm up the stairs to the bathroom, locking the door behind me. 'Bryony?' I hear him say, following me up the stairs. 'Bryony?'

I stand in the bathroom with my head in my hands. When I look up there is a mirror and I do not like what I see. A woman snarled with anger, irrational and crazy. I go to the loo, even though I don't need it. It is something to do that does not involve staring at my own, awful reflection.

Outside, I can hear Harry trying to talk to me. 'Did something happen at rehab?' he says, softly. I can hear he is on high alert, that he is almost permanently treading on eggshells, and I hate myself for it, another thing to add to the growing column of things I have against me. I wonder briefly if I am as bad as the boyfriend I once had who would erupt at any given moment, leaving bruises on my skin. The boyfriend I still, fifteen years later, had dreams about, my husband morphing into him and me realising, with horror, that I was stuck with this monster. But I was the monster now. I was the one to be feared.

'What happened?' repeats Harry, as I flush the loo.

How do I even begin to explain that what happened was . . . nothing. It was less than nothing. That what happened was he didn't immediately greet me at the door, wrapping me in hugs and telling me he loved me. How do I tell him that what happened was that he married a madwoman, that he impregnated a lunatic?

I unlock the door, and we are standing face to face in the hall. I start to cry. He bundles me into the spare room and I ask him again and again why he has stayed with me. Why he hasn't left. Why he didn't take Edie and get the hell out of here years ago. 'Tell me one reason why you stay with me,' I wail, in a way that I hope won't also wake up our daughter.

He shakes his head and takes a breath. 'I stay with you,' he says, 'because you are the most amazing person I have ever met.'

We stare at each other in the hallway. I tell him that he is the most amazing person *I* have ever met. It is the most unexpected moment of love, a thing that we can no longer take for granted. It is also too much for me to comprehend. I am overwhelmed with emotion. I go back to the bathroom and root around in the cabinet until I find a bottle of Night Nurse, which I swig from in the hope it will knock me out. It works. For the first time in what seems like forever, I sleep through the night in my husband's arms. I wake up feeling good, buoyant.

But this feeling is not warranted. It is a mistake.

The next day, I have a one-on-one with Peter. I tell him about what happened the night before. I tell him about the madness and the tears and what Harry said. I tell him that it felt like too much to take on, and that I had to knock myself out to get to sleep. After all the nights of insomnia, I needed a break, I needed to sleep soundly with my husband, so I took some Night Nurse. I tell him that I slept well for the first time since I had got sober, and that I had woken up feeling both physically and mentally closer to my husband. I expect Peter to be pleased for me. But instead his face looks very serious, as if I have just told him I have relapsed.

'Bryony,' he says, 'I need to just go back a bit there. I am really pleased that you feel closer to Harry, but did you say you took Night Nurse to knock yourself out?'

'Yes,' I say, very tentatively, starting to see what the problem was.

'OK,' he says, nodding his head. 'I'm afraid that counts as a using incident, which means I am going to have to suspend you.'

My jaw drops to the floor.

'The rules of the contract you signed are very clear. If you use alcohol and drugs, you will be suspended for twenty-four hours. And I'm afraid that taking Night Nurse to "knock yourself out"' – and here he uses quote fingers – 'counts as a using incident. So let me just be clear again. You didn't take the Night Nurse because you had a cold or the flu, did you?'

I shake my head, and feel some tears plop down into my lap.

'OK. I am sure you understand how serious this is.'

I don't, and I become defensive. 'It's not like I went out and got drunk,' I complain. 'I was exhausted and tired and I haven't slept for weeks now. I feel completely and utterly fucking *demented* at night, and there is only so much of it I – or my husband – can take. If I don't sleep properly soon I don't know how long I can stay sober for. I took the Night Nurse for the greater good, so I could rest and be ready to do recovery properly. It's not like drugs were even my thing!'

Peter shoots me a look. You know the kind of look. 'Weren't they?' He sounds surprised. 'Because for someone who claims that drugs weren't her thing, there are an awful lot of drugs in your story.'

For a moment, just a moment, I remember the time I accidentally overdosed on MDMA. It was my twenty-sixth birthday, and we had all gone to a pub in East London near my flat for a booze up. It was 4 p.m., and the sun was shining outside. My sister was there, and a load of my friends. I ordered the drinks safe in the knowledge that a mate had brought some coke with him. I settled in for the rest of the day. It was going to be epic. The friend with the drugs handed them to me, and I slunk off to the loo where I racked out a huge line of what I thought was cocaine. I snorted it greedily and as the powder shot up my nostrils I knew something wasn't right. It didn't feel like coke. It didn't smell like coke. It felt fruity rather than sharp. I left the bathroom and was intercepted by my friend before I could get back to the table. He saw the glazed look in my eyes.

'You saw that wasn't coke, right?' he said. 'You didn't take a coke-sized dose, did you?' I nodded my head and started to feel woozy. My friend started swearing. The pub started to spin and I started to leave my head. I was high above me, unable to get back to me, no matter how hard I tried. My sister was trying to get to me, too, but she wasn't managing it either. I could hear people saying, 'Is Bryony OK? Is everything OK?' And the next thing I knew I was back at my flat, and I was waking up sixteen hours later, feeling absolutely right as rain, my sister asleep on the living-room sofa after an all-night vigil over my bed. My friends had carried on, reasoning it was nothing to be worried about and that I had just had too much. They were right, but that didn't change the fact that I had, in my desperation to get high on coke, accidentally knocked myself out with ecstasy. I probably wasn't going to die but I certainly couldn't function and my birthday celebrations had – for me and my sister at least – ended before they had even really begun.

This episode occurred to me because Peter was right. Drugs did figure pretty regularly in my story, and if they didn't figure then it wasn't for want of trying. I would have snorted anything to stay awake and keep on drinking. Once, I even tried snorting gin, having heard it was quite the thing. It wasn't. And now, here I was in rehab, about to be suspended for taking *Night Nurse*. My desperation to get out of it was so all-encompassing that I would even resort to the stuff in my bathroom cabinet. What next? Cough mixture? Mouthwash? *Lighter fuel?* Peter was right to point out that my taking Night Nurse was a using incident, because it was. I had taken it not because I had a sore throat or a blocked nose, but because I wanted oblivion. Still, I had hoped that if I was to be suspended, it would be for something a little more exciting than some cold and flu medicine.

I became hysterical. I was hyperventilating. It was as if I was being expelled from school. I didn't know what I was going to say to my parents, or Harry. How would I explain it? How would I tell Holly? Would she be disappointed in me? Would a quiet judgement go around the room in group therapy that would be there until the end of my days, or at least the end of my days in rehab? I was mortified. Peter explained he was going to have to drug- and alcohol-test me. I sobbed silently in the room as he left to get the pot for me to piss in. How had it come to this? How had I been reduced to this quivering mess, weeping over a shot of Night Nurse, waiting to wee into a small plastic receptacle?

Peter returned with the necessary equipment. I felt that I had disappointed him, that he would be cross with me. I wept and wept, devastated at the idea of losing his approval. I knew, in that moment, that the opinion of others meant too much to me, but also that this was not something I could deal with right now. He told me that if the test came back clean, they would not have to suspend me, but I felt that I had somehow lost his trust, even though he had said nothing of the sort. I slunk off to the toilet, where I did what I had been told. I handed the warm pot to Peter, embarrassed and undone. He told me to wait in the hall while he went into the office. Three minutes later, he came out smiling. 'Your test came back clean, kiddo,' he said. 'So no suspension this time. But please don't see this as a behaviour that you should repeat. I'll see you tomorrow.'

There was a relief but there was also, once the terror of failure had gone, a reassuring knowledge. That I wanted this. That I wanted it so badly I would do anything to get it. I was not going to let some Night Nurse derail my attempts at getting sober. I left the centre and went straight to a meeting. In that moment of clarity, there wasn't anywhere else I would rather be. I marched in, and said hello to some of the now-familiar faces I had encountered at other twelve-step meetings around town. I sat down near the front and, as the meeting started, I breathed a sigh of relief. I was safe. For the first time in my life, I was safe, and I took comfort in the knowledge that the only person who could take that safety away was me.

8

Coming out

Eventually, though, it was time to leave the safe cocoon I had made for myself. The safe cocoon of rehab.

How had twelve weeks gone so slowly and yet so fast? How had something that had horrified me just months ago come to feel like home? I didn't want to leave Peter and Lisa and any of the other counsellors, but I couldn't stay here forever – not unless I fancied bankrupting myself, which I didn't.

It was coming up to Christmas, which is quite possibly the worst time for a recovering alcoholic to graduate from rehab. But at least Holly and I were graduating on almost the same day. At least we had each other. I didn't know if I could have got through the previous twelve weeks without her, or how I had managed the previous thirty-seven years without her.

'I think we might have hated each other if we'd have met while we were drinking,' I say one day.

'Why?' Holly seems offended. 'I think we would have had a right gas! Just think of the evenings out we could have had!' Briefly, we fall silent, and go misty-eyed at the thought of nights out we will never (hopefully) have.

'But we also might have killed each other. I think it's for the best that the drunk versions of ourselves never met.'

Holly nodded. A week before, we had encountered Blondie – the twenty-year-old we had met at the beginning of the programme – outside a pub near the rehab centre. She was slurring her words and clutching a glass of vodka. She had been thrown out of her flat for relapsing. Holly immediately took pity on her and offered her the spare room, which Blondie had gratefully, drunkenly accepted. But she had broken two vases, vomited on the kitchen worktop, and when she finally left, Holly having contacted her parents to explain the situation, we had found two empty bottles of cheap supermarket gin under the pillow.

It was a shock. The way Blondie behaved was completely different to the sweet, shy girl we had first encountered in treatment. But Peter explained that the

Blondie we were seeing was not the sober Blondie, and that they were in effect completely different people. It was a salutary lesson for us on how different we could be when drinking and using.

'I don't think I was ever *that* bad,' I said to Peter. He raised his eyebrows in a way that suggested I was very much mistaken, and I remembered what Harry had told me recently, about the nickname his flatmates had given me when we first got together: Santa Booze-A-Claus.

'There must have been times when my drinking was funny, surely?' I pleaded with Harry.

'Not really,' he smiled, ruffling my hair. 'Do you remember the laptop of mine you broke, spilling a bottle of wine over it?'

'Oh yeah,' I mumble, before changing the subject.

The thought of being this new version of myself excited me, but it was also terrifying. I could keep it up inside the confines of rehab, the weight of an £8,000 loan hanging over me, but I wondered how I would fare once I was in the outside world and had paid it back. My trust in myself was still tentative. I was scared of the Christmas party season, of Christmas full stop. I didn't know how I would cope when locked in a house with my family for two days. They were supportive of me and proud of me, but Christmas for them equalled wine and champagne, and there wasn't

a festive period in recent memory that hadn't ended
for me in blackout. But in recovery I was being taught
not to worry too much about things that hadn't
happened yet. 'Do you have to spend Christmas with
your parents today?' Peter asked me, when I raised my
concerns. I shook my head. 'So don't stress about it.'

The advice from Peter for dealing with Christmas
was this: 'Smile and wave. Just smile and wave. And
when you feel yourself about to pick an argument, ask
yourself: do you want to be happy, or do you want to
be right?'

I wanted to be both, if at all possible. But it was
good advice for life, generally, I felt.

On my last day of rehab, I realised I felt euphoric.
I had done something I had said I would do, had
completed something I had said I would complete. To
many people this might seem like nothing, like every
normal waking day. But to me it felt monumental. I
had not let anyone down. I had not let myself down.
For just over ninety days, I had not woken up and
immediately called myself a dick. I still wasn't sleeping
properly and my skin looked like the surface of the
moon, but I had stuck at this sobriety thing. I had
made a proper fist of it. The cravings were still there,
hitting me over the head at the most arbitrary moments
like a dead weight, a kettlebell, but I was finding I
was stronger than the cravings. There were, perhaps,

even little bits of me that I actually liked. Not many. Not heaps. But enough to keep me going for the time being.

Might it be possible, I wondered, to live a life free of the obsession of how awful I was? To wake up and just get on with my day without once stopping to flagellate myself?

I met the other inmates for coffee before my last rehab session, and ordered myself something to eat. I could not stop eating – it was as if a vast hunger had overtaken me. I was yet to have the spiritual awakening that so many people in recovery bang on about, but my stomach was awakening to food other than the bland stuff I had used merely to line my stomach before. Now I had begun to cook. The fridge had items inside it other than alcohol, and perhaps that in itself was enough of a miracle for me to be getting on with.

Arriving at rehab I was handed a pot to piss in. 'You weren't going to let me go without one last one of those!' I beamed to Peter. I practically skipped to the toilet, and went about my business. Then one last check-in, during which I was handed a special key ring to mark my graduation, followed by one last group therapy session. I felt emotional as the moments ticked past, but proud. When the session was over, I headed for the door and a celebratory dinner with Holly.

Peter stopped me on the way out. 'Would you mind coming into the office for a moment before you go?' I obliged, expecting him to offer me a private farewell. But instead he announced that my urine sample had tested positive for alcohol, and while I had graduated now and there was no way he could suspend me, he had to mention it.

I was flabbergasted.

'Have you been drinking, Bryony?'

'No,' I said. 'Absolutely not. Do you think I would turn up if I had?'

'You never know.'

I looked at Peter and I realised then that it must have been the food I had eaten before, a plate of pasta. We had been warned that the tests were highly sensitive – poppy seeds in bread could land you with a positive test for opium, while food cooked in wine could land you with a positive test for alcohol – and this was probably why I had failed my final urine test. But I also realised that just a month earlier, such an incident would have sent me into a tailspin. I would have worried about what he thought about me, and even gone so far as to doubt my own sanity in the process. Now I felt able to tell him coolly and calmly that it must have been something I ate.

'It could have been,' he smiled gently. 'And anyway, if you know in your heart that you haven't drunk alcohol, then you know you haven't drunk alcohol. And that's all that matters.'

He was right. I did know in my heart that I had not drunk any alcohol, and that I had absolutely no inclination to drink any alcohol, even if occasionally I was still beset by cravings. They were just cravings. They weren't going to kill me, and I was louder and more badass than them now. That trust in myself meant more to me than Peter could have ever known.

I hugged him, and left rehab with my head held high. It was remarkable. I may not have believed in a bearded man in the sky, but in twelve weeks, I had at least started to believe in me.

It was decided that I would see Peter once a week for the foreseeable future, which gave me a safety net. I needed one, given that I was fast realising, outside the security of rehab, that my life was in a state of absolute chaos. I had a marriage to repair, and a child to parent. I had a looming book deadline that had been put off when it became clear that . . . well, that I was an alcoholic. I was in debt. And I had a whole heap of apologies I felt I had to make to people now I realised what a nightmare I had been while drinking. It was interesting to me that not a single friend had been surprised when I wound up in rehab, that there did not appear to be one person who didn't think my getting sober was not a very good thing. Even my old drinking buddies approved, and wished me well in my endeavours. Everyone knew I could be trouble. They just didn't know, from my smiling face and boundlessly successful career, that I was also *in* a whole lot of trouble.

It wasn't as if my world had come crashing down. But its perspective had definitely altered. I began to notice things that had never occurred to me before, even though they were right there in front of me, hiding in plain sight. Had my drinking made my vision that blurry? I had never noticed the damp patches in the living-room ceiling, or the chipped paint on the walls. I had not noticed the cupboard door that was hanging off in the kitchen, or the thirty boxes of stuff we still hadn't unpacked in the spare room (we had moved in eighteen months previously). I hadn't noticed the piles of clean laundry in the corner of the bedroom that had taken on the form of a floordrobe given that I never put them away, and the piles and piles of unopened mail that had seemingly become one with the kitchen table.

My life was chaos. Even in the boring ways, it was chaos. I thought to myself: when did I last go to the dentist, or for a smear test? When had I last been to the opticians to get my eyes checked out? Did we have home insurance? Did we have any kind of insurance?

Was Edie up to date with her vaccinations? (She was, phew.) And where was her birth certificate? Did she even have a birth certificate? I supposed she must have, but I was stuffed if I could tell you where we kept it.

Normal life stuff had got in the way of my drinking so I had ignored it, and now my drinking was done the normal life stuff was making itself known. I had known that getting sober would force me to deal with my problems. I had no idea that they would also include household bills.

Someone also in sobriety told me it was like driving a car at ninety miles an hour, and then suddenly braking, only to find everything in the boot suddenly with you in the front seat. Or at least it would be if I had ever learnt to drive. Which, having been too busy being an alcoholic, I hadn't.

Was that something I was now going to have to do, too?

I was horrified that this chaos had existed forever, that I had only just started to see it now. It was like some sort of dreadful Magic Eye poster, the image of chaos only now emerging from the blurry background. Harry had done his best to keep things afloat, but he'd had a lot on his plate. Life had been overwhelming for him too. I could see, now, just how much work he had to do to keep us afloat – not just practically, but emotionally, too. It was a mistake to think that because he didn't often express emotions that he didn't actually feel them. I needed to start looking after my home and the people who lived in it. I needed to start doing my job.

The house was a mess. It was like the Old Curiosity Shop. One wrong move, and we would be buried under an avalanche of household bills.

I set about decluttering with a vigour that I had previously reserved only for drinking. I found all sorts of things that I had long ago given up hope of ever seeing again: that birth certificate; an expensive dress I had only worn once before losing; shreds, even, of my dignity. With each bin bag of detritus donated to the local charity shop or taken to the tip, I felt I was also shedding a bit of the shame of the past. I was being a proper grown-up, doing something that was befitting of a mum. The key to feeling like a competent adult with healthy self-esteem was simple, really: you just had to act like one.

There was a little bit of money left from the loan, which I immediately paid to a decorator so that he could put a lick of fresh paint over everything. I asked him to change the front door from boring blue to pale pink. If I could have scrubbed the walls of the memories of my drinking, I would have done. I fixed the garden gate, and changed light bulbs. I did all the things that Harry hadn't been able to in the desperate balancing act that was living with an alcoholic in active addiction. I picked up Edie every day from school, and organised play dates. At night I read with her for hours and hours, as many books as she wanted, each one a sort of apology for all the evenings I had prioritised alcohol over her.

I was now less frightened of telling the other mothers where I had been disappearing off to all this time. At the beginning it had all been so new to me – they had all been so new to me – and I was terrified of their judgement. But now I felt a little pride in myself for managing to give up drinking. I had not been to any of the parent nights out or the welcome drinks, and nobody had asked why – I guessed they had their own stuff to preoccupy them. It amazed me that, in this new, sober version of life, I had made friends with people who would never think of me as a drinker. People who might not ever know me to drink.

I told my doctor friend what I'd been up to, and her response blew me away. 'Wow,' she said, a tear forming in her eye. 'Just wow.' She came and hugged me. She held me tight. 'What you've done is amazing, Bryony. It's absolutely amazing. Thank you for telling me. It means so much to be in your trust.' It was the first time outside of rehab and the twelve-step meetings that I had not batted away something said sincerely, and it felt good. My cynicism was melting away. I felt like I did at the beginning of an evening, when I had just had a drink. There was the same glow that alcohol had given me, only with one crucial difference: this was real. It would stay with me forever, nourishing me instead of taking away.

There were other revelations, too.

So, so many revelations.

And questions. So, so many questions.

What, exactly, did you drink at a Christmas party when you were fresh out of recovery?

And if anybody at said Christmas party asked why you weren't drinking, what did you say?

How did you enjoy a Christmas party *without* drinking?

The answer was: you didn't. Not at first, anyway. You realised that life was not to be enjoyed all the time, that there were going to be some things you really didn't want to do but, for the sake of other people around you, you had to do. And that was fine. That was good. That was how life worked. I didn't have to do anything other than relax and go along with it.

Some old friends invited us to Christmas drinks. I felt excited to be heading out as my new, sober self. Excited and apprehensive. I wore high heels and tights and a dress, and shiny, dangly earrings, and I put on make-up knowing that I would take it off at the end of the night. I looked in the mirror and I smiled. It felt so alien, going out and knowing for sure that I was not going to make a fool of myself, that I would not try to score coke off the person I noticed was going to the loo all the time. This was my party trick, previously: I had an uncanny ability to sniff out the person who was as badly behaved as me.

I used to call December 'amateur's month'. All the people who had spent the rest of the year telling me they couldn't come out, or that they needed to get home early, suddenly came crawling out of the wood-work. They wanted to party with me, to go out on the town. Where had these people been in the cold, unfor-giving months of February and March? Where had they been when I really needed them in January, for that matter? Doing their boring exercise in abstinence, while I continued on as normal. By December, when they all re-emerged wanting a bit of fun-time Bryony, I was exhausted. I was all partied out. I no more wanted to stick a pair of Christmas baubles on my ears and go dancing than I did learn Mandarin.

But I was selfless, and I was also, more importantly, an alcoholic, so I obliged. I was an enabler. I was an excuser. With me by their side they could behave as badly as they wanted and not feel in the slightest bit embarrassed because I had probably done something even worse in my time, if not that night. 'I don't know how you do this all year round!' they would shout into my ear, usually about 2 a.m., when we had found ourselves moving on from the Christmas party to some awful dive bar that was still open. God, there were so many dive bars, most of them illegal, no doubt. Pre-Harry, I had once found myself in Shoreditch, in a sort of speakeasy high up on the roof of a building I could not in a million years direct you to now. People were openly taking drugs. It was like something out of a movie, or maybe that was just my imagination. Maybe it was a bit grottier, more like something out of a Hogarth painting.

I had started snogging some man, and even though he had told me his name over and over again, I could not for the life of me remember it. I was so out of it that all the information relayed to me went straight in one ear, through my jellied brain and out the other. I kept breaking off from our snogging and asking him what his name was. I would apologise. 'I'm terribly sorry, but *who are you?*' Eventually he walked off, and I ended up chatting to a couple, whose names also evaded me. They invited me home. I snogged them, too, and things progressed to the bedroom, but eventually I realised they were so into each other that they weren't all that interested in me, and I slunk out the door, the horror of being left out of a drunken threesome sobering me right up.

The self-loathing that had plagued me after the event confused me now I was sober. Does it really matter who I'd slept with, as long as it was both consensual and legal? But my shame had always found any number of ways to make itself known. I had been ashamed simply to exist. Ashamed just to be me.

But now? Well now, I wasn't. Those feelings felt so very far away from the person I was today. My sobriety felt like a sort of super power. It made me feel strong and steadfast. Being sober at a party was, ironically, after all that, the coolest I had ever felt on the social scene. I did not need alcohol and drugs to walk into a joint with my head held high. I may have done to procure a threesome, but for some reason crazy sex had stopped interesting me quite so much since I had stopped taking drugs. I could fantasise about it, if I wanted, but I was too contained and content to actually want it. I felt for the first time that all that sexual shame was behind me. I did not have to be embarrassed about my wants or needs. I just needed to be comfortable enough in myself that I could satisfy them in a way that didn't involve blacking out or betraying Harry or taking illegal drugs and putting myself in danger.

Harry and I had agreed that we wouldn't stay at the party past 9.30 p.m. He wouldn't drink in solidarity with me. If it got too much, I would pretend that the babysitter had texted announcing some sort of minor emergency: a fever perhaps, or a leaking pipe. With these rules in place I felt safe.

We were the first to arrive at the party. It wasn't cool but it did at least excuse us if we were the first to leave. My friends hugged us and welcomed us into their fabulous home. I felt briefly as if I was in *Love Actually*. Harry had brought with him a bottle of red wine which he handed over to our hosts immediately, as if to get rid of it. They thanked us, and then they offered Harry a glass of champagne and me a glass of sparkling elderflower, explaining that they had bought it for me especially. I was touched by the gesture, and relieved, and though it tasted repulsively sweet I drank it anyway in gratitude.

As the party warmed up I felt an immeasurable sense of pride in my sobriety. Perhaps the sugar in the elderflower was making me high, but I could not stop talking about it to anyone who asked, and I could not stop talking about it to a fair few who didn't. Some people smiled politely and changed the subject, while others wanted to know all the gory details. Was that it, then? Would I never, ever drink again? Not ever? Could I not even have one? Did rehab not teach you to drink sensibly? Oh wow, people chimed. The universal agreement was that they could never do that.

But then, they didn't have to. They were people for

whom a glass of wine at night was a nice accompaniment to dinner. Whereas I was someone for whom three bottles of wine at night was a nice replacement for dinner. I couldn't help but notice how very slowly everyone drank. I spoke to one woman for a whole twenty minutes without her taking a single sip from her flute of champagne. I barely registered a word she said, such was my astonishment at her abstinence. The champagne was going to get warm and flat. I wanted to shake her and tell her to drink it immediately.

I wanted to shake everyone. '*Drink!*' I wanted to shout. 'You're allowed to drink, so why aren't you drinking *properly*?'

There were people who put their hands over their glasses when someone tried to top them up. There were people who only drank one glass, very slowly, because they had a long drive the next day and needed to be fresh. There were people who turned down champagne because it gave them migraines (so what! Just drink more!), and there were people who turned down champagne because they were exhausted after a week at work and they'd better not. There were people who chatted with one another animatedly without clutching a glass in their hand. There were people who chatted with one another animatedly while clutching a glass in their hand, but they did not seem to be looking over one another's shoulder to see where

208

their next top up would come from. There were people who had one glass of fizz and then left because they had promised they'd be home to cook their teenage children dinner, and there were people for whom this whole evening was not about getting as drunk as possible.

It was astonishing. It was like watching a David Attenborough documentary unfold. All these fascinating, curious human beings I did not know existed until now! And this information was useful. I knew that it was not within my gift to drink like these people. I knew that I didn't want to drink like these people. I knew that I was doing the right thing. This was my life, now. I didn't drink I didn't drink I didn't drink.

My God. I didn't drink.

Well, I mean I did drink. Of course I drank. Everyone had to drink. I just didn't drink alcohol.

How had the verb 'to drink' been colonised by alcohol? What about those of us who chose not to drink alcohol? We were people too, with hydration needs! And yet I frequently found myself needing to explain that while I did drink liquid, I didn't drink alcohol. Oh, people would say. Why? They didn't want to ask if I was pregnant, as this would seem too rude, so they usually asked if I was on antibiotics. I came up with all sorts of explanations at first, to stop their questions. My favourite was that I had drunk my life-time's allowance of alcohol by the time I reached thirty-seven, and several other people's allowances, too. But in time it just became easier to tell them the truth. I didn't drink because I was an alcoholic.

That usually shut them up.

There were some people who were apologetic for their own drinking, even though they needn't have been. We would meet people for lunch at a pub, and as they automatically went to order a glass of wine they would suddenly stop, and look to me for permission to carry on. 'Is it OK?' they would say, sweetly, politely. 'It's really not a problem if you'd rather we didn't.' But I actively encouraged these displays of normal drinking. I found them educational and insightful. I did not think I could sit and watch a group of friends on a huge night out, but to see the normal drinker in their natural habitat was a useful thing for me. It reminded me why I was doing what I was doing. For me, none really was a hell of a lot easier than one.

None of this solved the problem of what to drink at social occasions. There has been a boom in non-alcoholic beverages, but Peter explained that non-alcoholic beverages were for non-alcoholics. They tasted like alcohol but they were not alcohol, and it wasn't worth the risk. Had I drunk beer for its taste?

No. I had drunk beer for the buzz it gave me, and there wasn't any point reminding myself of that buzz. It was seductive, and might lead me to the real thing.

Fizzy drinks like lemonade and Coca-Cola made my stomach turn. I was still drinking fluids in the volumes I had in active addiction – I may not have been a drinker, but I was still very much an alcoholic, and could not quite shake that desire to order the largest of everything. Five pints of lemonade was not an option, though – not if I wanted to keep my teeth. Tonic water reminded me too much of spirits. Seedlip, the trendy faux spirit that everyone was banging on about, cost more per litre than liquid gold. And as for elderflower, the perennial drinks-party offering for teetotallers . . . well, I was a recovering alcoholic, not a fucking wood sprite.

I stuck to water. I stayed close to the canapés. If I wasn't going to drink the host's booze then I was definitely going to eat their food. I smoked copiously. I did what I had to do. Life was showing me glorious things every day, and I needed to stay sober to see them.

I had assumed that the spiritual awakening that is so central to recovery from addiction would involve bright lights at the end of a tunnel. Perhaps there would be angels singing beautiful songs and playing lutes. Maybe

I would leave my body, travel high above it and see the wonder of the world. Or perhaps I would hear God call to me in a transcendental moment of divinity. Something like that.

I hadn't bargained on it involving banana bread.

I don't know if you've worked this out yet, but I am not exactly a whizz in the kitchen. I'm not exactly a whizz *anywhere*. My mum was a feminist who worked hard and equated the kitchen with the chains of the patriarchy. Or at least that was what she told me. Maybe she just didn't have the time to teach us to cook. Whatever the case, we were brought up believing that there were way more fun things that girls could be doing than baking. Like, I don't know, drinking. So I wore my inability to make anything more complicated than a spaghetti Bolognese as a sort of feminist badge of honour, when in reality I was using this feminist badge of honour as cover for the fact that the only thing I wanted to do in my spare time was drink. Hobbies and interests were never my strong point, and I developed a deep-seated disdain for people who had them as a way to justify my increasingly skin-deep existence.

I remember working with a lovely girl who was a few years younger than me, and every Monday she would appear bright-eyed and bushy-tailed with a Tupperware container crammed full of baked goods. She was sweet and kind, but my mind boggled at the kind of person you would have to be to spend your Sunday baking for colleagues like me, who had spent their Sunday doing what, exactly? Lying in their own sweat and self-loathing after a two-night bender, no doubt.

But in sobriety I was realising that so many of the things I claimed to despise were actually things that I hankered after desperately. Safety. Security. The ability to nourish and look after myself. A friend I had made in sobriety had told me that if you wanted good self-esteem, then the easiest way to go about it was to do estimable things, and being able to provide food for yourself and your family was a pretty basic estimable thing that I had so far failed to do.

The whole point of life was to experience it, surely? And yet I had not been experiencing it at all. It was ironic that the need to experience life was what had led me to alcohol in the first place – the lure of a magic tincture that could deaden my fears and anxiety so I could, for a few hours, feel the way everyone else did. But I was learning that there was no one way that everyone else felt, that everyone else was battling their own fears and anxieties – it was just that some people chose to quell them with baking while others chose to quell them with booze. I had fallen into the latter camp, and where had it led me? To isolation and desper-ation and, ultimately, rehab. And now I was out, I didn't want to isolate myself any more. I didn't want to keep pretending that the way I had been living my life had made me in any way happy.

So I bought a kids' baking book. And I had that spiritual awakening I had been waiting for.

Baking was not like cooking, which I could just about manage in that it only really involved chucking a random assortment of whatever you wanted into a pan and waiting for it to heat up. Baking was measured. It was precise. It was exact. Baking was everything I wasn't, and on the one occasion I had attempted it in a crack at acting the perfect mother, way back before I was sober, it had been an unmitigated disaster. I had ignored the recipe I had googled on my phone, unsure what any of the measurements meant or what bicarbonate of soda was. Willy nilly, I had gone about this baking endeavour in my own chaotic way, and the result was not surprisingly a mess. It was like a metaphor for my life. And now I wanted to change the metaphor.

Back then I had set about making angel-shaped biscuits for Christmas. That seemed simple enough, but it wasn't, and so now I decided to start with the very basics. There was no point trying to run before I could walk, and in the moment of realising that I felt slightly flabbergasted by how sensible I was being. Sensible. Me! It was a wonderful feeling, a pleasing feeling, a Mary Poppins kind of feeling. I announced to Edie that we were making banana bread, and she shook her head in memory of our last culinary outing. But I had expected this, and as a way to encourage her had purchased a mini apron covered in unicorns as a gift, along with the ingredients. Her eyes lit up, and in a shot she was in the kitchen.

Christmas was coming, so I put festive songs on the radio. We danced around to 'Frosty the Snowman' as we followed the recipe to the letter, and the number: three eggs, three bananas, 375 grams of flour, two teaspoons of baking powder, one teaspoon of salt, 125 millilitres of vegetable oil, 200 grams of sugar, two teaspoons of vanilla extract, plenty of butter. We whisked and we licked spoons and we laughed together. 'It's the Most Wonderful Time of the Year' came on and I thought my heart was going to burst with joy. We spilt flour everywhere, and as I went to clean it up I am afraid I was hit with a pang of relief that the white powder in front of me was not cocaine. I could have cried in that moment, cried shiny tears of absolute joy. I was baking with my daughter and we were safe and in this bubble of baking nothing could touch us. Not one thing.

We poured the mixture into the loaf tins – I owned loaf tins, and today I had learnt how to grease them! – and put them in the oven. Together, we sat cross-legged on the floor of the kitchen watching the banana bread rise from the tins, licking the side of the bowl, the combination of that and the smell wafting up our nostrils making us giddy with excitement. And in that moment my body felt as warm as the oven I was watching. I felt, in a sense, high with happiness. What was more, I had made myself happy without having to do anything illegal, or anything that demeaned me. As we watched the banana bread bake, Christmas songs still playing in the background, I realised I was having my spiritual awakening. It was here and it was in my kitchen and there were no angels or shining lights or callings from God. Just the knowledge that it was possible to find in the ordinary, things that were absolutely, gobsmackingly extraordinary.

But just as important as the things I had started doing were the things I had stopped doing. Drinking was the obvious one, but there were plenty more subtle shifts of abstinence. I would be going about my business – having a play date, a bath, going for a run – when I would suddenly remember how perpetually anxious I used to feel. It would suddenly occur to me – an epiphany, another spiritual awakening if you like – that I no longer lived in a constant state of despair.

I no longer worried all the time that I was dying. Health anxiety had been a constant – I worried that my drinking had destroyed my body, and that I was going to expire at any given moment. I would sit there in the evening, in the garden, a packet of fags and a huge bottle of beer in front of me, and I would ask my husband if the tightness I felt in my chest or the pain I had in my left arm were the signs of a heart attack. 'Of course not,' he would reassure me, because what else could he do when faced with a woman who was never going to listen to him anyway? The only way I knew to stop the anxiety and the feelings of panic about my impending death was to drink more of the poison I feared had poisoned me in the first place. It was madness. But then I was mad.

Since becoming sober, I hadn't been to the doctor to ask them if I had liver disease or lung cancer or if I was at risk of having a heart attack.

I hadn't spent £200 going to an emergency dentist to check if I had mouth cancer.

I hadn't painstakingly counted the paracetamol in the house, to check I hadn't taken an overdose in the night that I had forgotten about.

I hadn't thought about taking an overdose.

I hadn't asked my husband if he thought it was possible I had killed someone in the night, or molested our own child, and blanked it out in horror.

And nor had I asked him if he thought it possible I might have left the house in the dead of night, slept with a stranger and contracted a terrible disease.

I hadn't texted anyone to ask if they hated me, or if I had done something wrong.

I hadn't woken up and immediately thrown up in fear.

I hadn't put myself or my family at risk.

I hadn't been unable to leave the house because I was scared I would leave the iron on or a candle blazing and it was just simpler to stay put.

My OCD had existed before I had started drinking, but the alcohol had exacerbated it, and now I had stopped throwing petrol on the fire, the fire had died down and my mind had finally reached a state of peace. And into the vacuum left by all the anxieties and fears I felt before had fallen a desire to bake and exercise and parent well. It was all related. The bad things I no longer did were responsible for the good things I now did. As loath as I was to admit it, Peter had been right when he spoke about the effect of alcohol on the brain's chemistry. The smile of a child really was all it took to make me happy, and the dawn chorus of birds was a reason to celebrate, not hide. I was waking up to the birds, not going to sleep to them. I had started to turn my life around, away from the dark, and with every nudge in its new direction I lapped up the feeling of the warm sun on my face and wondered how I had ever managed to live without it.

*

I was worried about Christmas because all my experiences of Christmas had been worrying, at least on the alcohol front. There was the Christmas I ruined by taking my then fifteen-year-old sister out on an all-night bender, returning in the early hours and waking the whole house up as we took turns to vomit in the loo. There was the Christmas I sat sullenly at my aunt's, demanding more and more booze until eventually my mum was forced to take me home, cutting the festivities short.

There was the Christmas I had left, at 5 p.m. on the dot, so I could go to a friend's house round the corner and take shed loads of cocaine. I had returned at 11 a.m. on Boxing Day, my mother white with fear. There was the Christmas where I had drunkenly upended the trestle table my mum had had to buy to fit everyone around for the turkey. We had all been covered in red wine and white sauce. And then there was the Christmas when I had gone out every night for seventeen nights in a row, and left all my shopping until 24 December. I went to Oxford Street, which was my first mistake (or was it my second or third or five hundredth?) and, overwhelmed with people and a fortnight and a half's worth of hangovers, I had had a funny turn. I thought I was having a stroke, and told the St Johns Ambulance crew parked helpfully outside Liberty's as much. They told me that I had just overdone it, perhaps, and sent me home. Nobody got any presents that year, at least not from me, just IOUs and the promise of a good time.

But I realised, as my first adult sober Christmas approached, that I had nothing to worry about. I had nothing to worry about because the common denominator of all these ruined Christmasses was me consuming alcohol, and now that the alcohol had been taken out of the mix, things should return to normal. I couldn't stop anyone else from drinking, but I could remember that watching everyone else drinking was not going to kill me.

On Christmas morning, I watched my daughter open her stocking and I did not feel resentful that I had been woken up at 6 a.m. and nor did I feel like I was going to be sick. I paid attention to every toy and book she pulled from her stocking, and made noises of delight to match hers. Afterwards, I excused myself and went to town to make the tea for an hour at an all-day twelve-step meeting. This organisation was amazing in the support it offered people, and the least I could do was offer a little bit of support back. Two hours later, my tea shift done and a meeting taken in, I went and met Harry and Edie around the corner in a park. Then we walked together to a nearby restaurant where we met the rest of my family for Christmas lunch. We had decided this year that it was safest to take

Christmas out of the house, so the house could be a safe sanctuary to return to. And so it was that I enjoyed the calmest Christmas of my life.

I realised, as we ate, that nobody in the family drank like I did. There was a flute of champagne here, a glass of red wine there, but otherwise everyone else focused on the food and the presents. It occurred to me that maybe they were being restrained in respect of my sobriety, and I took a moment to thank them if that was the case. 'We're just so proud of you,' said my dad, raising his glass of red wine to me. I laughed at the gesture, while my sister and brother and mother chimed in with their agreements. Could it be that I had been forcing them to drink all this time?

I remembered Christmasses where I had been annoyed, even as an adult, that my mum had bought my sister something I wanted, when I had counted up the tally of presents between us from my parents even though I was in my thirties. Presents, and booze, had been the point of Christmas. It was pathetic. Now I felt no need for presents. I would appreciate whatever had been bought for me, and enjoy the company of my family. It was cheesy and twee and it would have made the Bryony of a year before vomit with cynicism. But the Bryony of a year before was in the past now, and as I turned to look at her, I felt a real sadness for her. She had made her world so tiny and small, and now it was beginning to get big again. Really big. We all cycled back to our house on Boris bikes, where I fed the banana bread to my extended family and we opened presents and I remembered that the best gift I would ever receive was sobriety – nothing could top it, no diamond or handbag or flashy holiday.

9

Choose life

The clock chimed midnight on a new year, and I had no memory of it. I had no memory of it not for the usual reasons – most years had begun in a blur – but because I had fallen asleep next to my daughter hours before, reading her stories and stroking her back before being sucked into slumber myself. I had set a silent resolution for myself, that I would take my time with this precious human, and give her the attention she had always deserved but not always received. The truth of my illness washed over me as I lay with her back tucked into my body, her eyelids fluttering as I stroked her forehead. I had always told myself that she was the most important thing in my life, that my love for her was all-encompassing. But alcoholism had made

223

a mockery of this, and I realised that in reality, my daughter had spent the first four years of her life playing second fiddle to my drinking. She had not been the most important thing in my life. Alcohol had.

This simple but stark fact winded me on an almost daily basis. I wanted to use its force to turn back time and do everything again. I wanted to take myself back to the delivery suite, to whisper into my morphined ear that whatever I did, I should never, ever pick up an alcoholic drink again. But I couldn't, so instead I used its power to propel me forward. All that mattered was that she was my priority now. I could only hope that I had made these changes soon enough, and that she would have no memory of Drunk Mummy, who would hurry her to bed so she could go on the lash.

Plus, it was Dry January, that period of the year when everyone gave up booze for the good of their health, and I figured that this widespread temperance would be helpful in my own quest to stay sober. Suddenly, I would be on the same page as everyone else, and that had to be a good thing, right?

But I soon realised that I was not on the same page as everyone else. I was not on the same page as the people who could take or leave booze for long periods of time, the people who could pick it back up again in February, like thirty-one days without drinking was no big deal. Nothing at all! I was not on the same page as the 'sober curious' people who announced on Instagram that they had never been big drinkers, yet still they had noticed a difference for giving up their weekly glass of red wine. Oh, how I wanted to throttle these people for taking a very real problem that was *mine* and somehow making it *theirs*. I knew that this irritation was not rational, that anyone seen to be embracing the alcohol-free movement should be applauded, but I wanted them to pipe down and not rub their virtuousness in my face. I wanted them to *fuck off*, if truth be told.

I was also not on the same page as the people who joked to me that given they found Dry January hard, they could never do what I had done in giving it up *forever*. They were trying to let me know how they admired me, how strong they thought I was, but I only felt weak for finding myself in this situation where I had behaved so badly that all of my booze privileges had been taken away from me. I wanted to shout at them that I didn't find this easy, that I found being sober really, really HARD, but that it wasn't as hard as the alternative, which was killing myself slowly with the very thing that I thought was keeping me alive. I wasn't even on the same page as Harry who, having junked the booze in solidarity, was now back to his one glass a night, an idea so alien that it almost made me think we were from different planets.

Dry January came and Dry January went and I could not escape the fact that whatever time of year it was, I was always left with the exhausting business of being myself. But I had Holly. Holly was such a gift, such a joy. In my friendship with her, I was learning for the first time about relationships completely free of judgement, instead filled with understanding. Culturally I had had it drummed into me that the most meaningful relationship of my life would be a romantic one. And while my relationship with Harry was undoubtedly important – how wonderful it was to have sobered up and realised I was married to an absolute star, rather than an abusive arsehole, as many people did – I was realising that *the* most important relationship I would have, the one that would help all the other ones survive, was the one with myself. Recovery, I realised, was in many ways a feminist act of defiance, a stripping back of all the patriarchal ways I had come to quiet my supposedly 'unfeminine' behaviours – don't be hysterical (express emotions) or loud (express opinions); just sit quietly and numbly without feeling. With Holly I was able to recognise these patterns and see them for what they were; what's more, I was able finally to fight against them. We were a two-woman girl gang, reclaiming our voices after decades of drowning them with drink.

I *was* on the same page as Holly, and I realised that

I was so lucky to have this, that to be on the same page with just one person was enough, because when you had one person on the same page as you, it didn't matter quite so much that you weren't on the same page as anybody else. To be understood and accepted so absolutely was to be seen, and to be seen was to start the process of forgiveness of one's self. I knew that this process was not one way, that Holly was also receiving from me what I was receiving from her, and this somehow made it all the more profound. Life, I was learning, was just as much about giving as it was about receiving. Like Holly and me, the two could not exist properly without each other.

It is generally accepted that for the first year of recovery, you should try not to do too much. You take it easy. You attempt to relax into sobriety. You don't make any major life changes – renouncing alcohol is enough to be getting on with for the time being. Alcoholics and addicts, explained Peter, have a habit of taking on too much, of thinking they can do everything, and this can lead to overwhelm and possible relapse.

Relapse. It was the word everyone feared, the word that would reset every hard-earned day of your sobriety clock back down to zero. Just one sip of alcohol, and it was gone.

But I felt an unstoppable energy inside me, the

unstoppable energy that comes from knowing you are lucky to be alive. I could take nothing for granted, not my being, not the breath inside me, not the conscious knowledge inside my brain that I was constantly seeking to bolster after a lifetime seeking to destroy it. I had started to read about the miracles of science, of the brain and the body and the universe. I discovered the incredible good fortune we experienced by even being born – an improbability so vanishingly small that there was more chance of the dinosaurs roaming the earth again, or England winning a football World Cup. First, your biological parents had to meet. Then they had to choose to have sex, which led to your biological father releasing millions of sperm into your biological mother's body, any one of which could lead to millions of different human outcomes. With a slight change of condition – your parents were disturbed by a door-bell, or your dad says something that pissed your mum off and caused her to call a halt to proceedings – and your shot at life is gone. You could be a whole different person. The sperm that made you had to battle through a veritable obstacle course of conditions, aiming to whittle out the weak – natural acids, uphill distances the equivalent of a sperm IronMan, white blood cells protecting your mother's egg like nightclub bouncers, if indeed your mother's egg was even there.

Then, if you beat the odds and managed to grow

from fertilised egg into a foetus, you had to avoid the very real threats of miscarriage or stillbirth and make it until the day you are born, which is, according to many doctors, the most dangerous day of your life. Once safely delivered, you then have to stay alive every day, and it was here that I *really* realised I had beaten the odds. For as soon as I had picked up alcohol, as soon as I had started drinking it to excess and begun dabbling with cocaine, I was essentially playing Russian roulette. I had experienced health anxiety, sure, but I had never really accepted the absolute danger I put my body in every time I drank to black out or mixed alcohol with cocaine. If I had, I would have stopped much earlier.

There were hundreds and hundreds of occasions that I could not remember because of my drinking. Occasions when anything could have happened to me, occasions when things probably did. It was only now that I could see the very fine line that existed between coming home from a night out safely, and not coming home at all. The mugging, the footprint on my pants, the vague flashbacks of strange men looming over me in dark staircases – it was not worth thinking about any of these things, because they were done, in a faraway and dark past, but I could at least use them as motivation to prevent things like this ever happening again.

I remembered the times when I had come down from my binges, my temperature falling as my whole body shook and shivered under the duvet. If I looked in the mirror and sniffed, I could see the effects of my drug use in the way my right nostril caved further than the left one, the cartilage weakened by that particular nostril being my chosen one to snort through. Sometimes I would stick a cotton bud up my nose, to check if the cocaine had eroded a hole in my septum. This was the kind of horror effect of cocaine I had read about in magazine articles about soap actresses and rock stars and socialites who had become addicted to the drug. My septum was, thankfully, fine, but all the time I had been using, the combination of alcohol and cocaine had created a deadly chemical known as cocaethylene, which could cause severe heart and liver damage over time. When I read about its effects, about the dangers I had put myself in, I realised how lucky I was. How lucky I was to have survived, and how lucky I was to have found a path to sobriety.

I felt as if I had escaped death. Life had chosen me, and now I was going to choose life. I was going to choose it *hard*. It was beautiful, it was wondrous, it was *here*, and now I had realised this I had to fill it with as much stuff as possible. It was the least I could do to show thanks for this insanely epic gift I had been given.

*

I had an energy that would not go away. I started writing a book about running, finishing it in miracle time and diving headfirst into its promotion. I would do anything, anything asked of me! I was asked to judge a book prize, which rewarded excellent writing about health and medicine in literature. It would involve reading fifty books in a little under two months, but hey, I could do it! I took delivery of all the books, piled them up in my living room, and sat cross-legged on the floor in front of them in a sort of awe. There were books about junior doctors, books about Spanish flu, books about dementia. There were memoirs about motor neurone disease, memoirs about addiction, memoirs about being brought up in the care system. I puffed out my cheeks and let out a huge breath at the enormity of what I had taken on, but I felt a huge gratitude, too. I set about reading with abandon.

I gobbled up a book about the vagaries of Victorian medicine. This was the kind of thing that I would never, ever have been open to reading before, and in my drinking I doubt I would have agreed to be a judge on this prize. It would have got in the way of my boozing – my reading back then was sporadic, at best, and I would often lack the concentration or indeed the consciousness to make it through more than one page. Books were bought not to be read, but to be displayed on shelves as a grand show of my intelligence. Now I was averaging a book a day. It was amazing. It was fascinating. I felt, with each page I turned, that my world was getting bigger and bigger and bigger, and my brain was getting brighter and brighter and brighter. Every discovery was a joy, every fact something to be repeated over dinner to Harry.

The amazing discoveries I was making were not only to be found in books. They were also to be found in the banana bread moments, the seemingly mundane instances of life that had eluded me and that I now wanted to experience with a passion that might have seemed slightly at odds with their dull practicality. I felt as if I were on a fact-finding mission, the mission being to find out things that normal non-alcoholics knew from birth, but that had somehow passed me by, so immersed was I in my inebriation. Did you know that there was a company called Ocado that delivered supermarket food to your door? Did you know that there were millions of box sets you could watch for hours every evening? Did you know that there were places called dry cleaners where you could take your musty, dirty winter coats? Did you know that in the morning there was a radio show called the *Today* programme, that you could listen to in order to find out what was going on in the world? Did you know there were museums you could visit, and art galleries you could attend, and theatre shows you could watch?

I had been vaguely aware of all of these things when I was drinking, but I had dismissed them out of hand as too boring and too tedious for a life as wild as mine. A ha. A ha ha ha! Now, as the months of sobriety flew by and I flew high, I realised how very wonderful these things were. How very wonderful everything was. Life was incredible! Life was astonishing! And I wanted to enjoy every last beautiful, boring bit of it.

At around four months sober, my boss asked if I wanted to go to the Maldives for a week to review a new hotel there. I could bring my husband and daughter if I wanted – all I would have to do was pay for the flights. I didn't really have the money for said flights, but it seemed like too good an opportunity to turn down, so I found ways of making it work. We all deserved a bit of a holiday after everything, and how often do you get offered free accommodation at a resort in the Indian Ocean in January?

We had been to the Maldives before, on a belated honeymoon. Edie was ten months old and came with us. I don't remember that much of it, because I spent most of my time enjoying the free childcare and the ice-cold beer. The stand-out moment had been drunkenly wiggling a cotton bud in my ear and bursting my ear drum, meaning I couldn't go snorkelling and see any of the amazing marine life. Did I care? Not really, as long as there was a babysitting service and fine wines.

The amount I had taken for granted sent shockwaves through me. How could I have squandered so much? Now, as we set off for our return visit, I was determined not to do the same.

That was easier said than done, because holidays for me had been all about the booze, the one time of the year when you were basically expected to drink all day. 'You're on holiday!' people would say, and that was all it took – I was off. Holidays provided the perfect foil for my alcoholism. I could shrug off hangovers under a pair of sunglasses on a lounger, and a sunset always looked better framed by a tall glass of something bubbly. Speaking of sunsets, there was not a single one I had experienced on a holiday that hadn't been set to a sundowner – huge tumblers of beer in the Caribbean, margaritas in Spain. As for sunrises, well, if I had seen one that I remembered then it was only because of the crushing sense of anxiety I'd felt at still being up.

But this was going to be different. I just knew it.

On our first morning, I woke up at 5 a.m. to the sound of birds. Harry and Edie were still fast asleep, so I put on my trainers and went for a run around the island. This was the pattern that our days would take: me running, or signing up to an early-morning yoga class, before meeting my family for breakfast. Then we would go swimming, maybe go out with Edie on a boat to see dolphins, or walk along the shore to look at the baby sharks. Then lunch, then some kids' club activity that I felt compelled to join – crafting, face painting, a treasure hunt of some sort. Then more swimming, more lounging, followed by dinner and an early night. And then it would all start again.

On those early mornings, when I woke before everyone else and went down to the beach to watch the sun rise, I thought about all the times I had been away and fucked things up because of my drinking. The visit to New York, when I got so drunk that my friend had to come and wake me up and pack my bags so we didn't miss our flight. The flight to Beijing, where the cabin crew had been forced to invite me into the galley and suggest that I might have had enough. The time in Nairobi when I had visited a friend and gone for a night out with her, only to somehow, drunkenly, get separated from her, and spend several hours wandering around with not a clue where I was. The time in Mombasa, a week later, when I became ill and dehydrated on her wedding day not because of some bug, but because of how much beer I had drunk and sun I had got. The time in Spain, when I had gone off with some Australian backpacker who was handsome but was also smoking crack, and ended up in a nightclub where porn was projected onto the walls. The occasion I went to Los Angeles for work for just forty-eight hours, thirty-six of those forty-eight hours spent on a cocaine binge with the PR I had travelled with. The time I was supposed to be going to Morocco for work, but got so drunk at home the night before that I missed my flight. There were enough stories like this to fill an entire book – moments where I had been privileged enough, through my work, to travel to amazing places, but that, through my alcoholism, I had failed to see at all. They were nothing more than stamps in my passport, if indeed I could find my passport. More often than not it was lost, and I would find myself traipsing to the emergency office in central London, spending money I didn't have to get a new one.

So each sober sunrise and sunset felt like a miracle I had to witness. I felt sad that I had missed so many in my life, that the world had been turning all along, doing its magic thing, and I'd been too pissed to notice. Whereas just months ago the sun rising and the birds calling had had the power to send me into despair, now they filled me with joy. Everything meant something now. I wanted to gobble it all up, with the same enthusiasm I had once gobbled up alcohol and drugs.

In sobriety, I was learning that I was not the gregarious party girl I had thought I was. In my drinking days I was the life and soul of the party, or at least I was the life of the party, having had very little soul. Now I just wanted to hide quietly in the corner of one, if I absolutely had to go to it. It was peculiar, at the age of thirty-seven, to discover you're not actually the person you thought you were, that everything you had assumed to be true about yourself had turned out to be completely false. Alcohol had given me Dutch courage. But sobriety had made me properly brave.

I had been given life, but what could I give life in return? I decided to say yes to everything, even if it was not practical. I was offered another place on the London Marathon, so I took it. If I had managed to run 26.2 miles while drinking, imagine how wonderful it would be sober? I teamed up with my friend Jada, a plus-size model and activist, who was running her first marathon and had asked if we could do it together. We started training, two size eighteen girls showing the world that we could, and it was on one of these training runs that I came up with an idea. 'Why don't we run the marathon in our underwear?' I suggested to Jada. 'To show people that runners' bodies really do come in every shape and size, that the only thing holding most people back is themselves.' To my surprise, she didn't laugh it off. In fact, she agreed. And so it was that my bog-standard marathon turned into a practically naked marathon.

It didn't scare me. My body had appalled me for years and years, and I had treated it terribly. It had been through enough. Now I felt proud of it and I wanted to show the world, or at least the streets of London, what was possible. I had been through rehab, I had got myself sober, and running 26.2 miles in only my underwear was nothing in comparison.

I weighed fifteen stone. Stretch marks ran down my stomach and my thighs. Cellulite dimpled every available surface. The scar from my emergency caesarean section ran across my pelvis. My boobs were huge, grotesque purple balloons in the process of deflating themselves. Had I thought this through? Yes, yes I had. Because despite all of this, my body had kept me alive all these years when it really shouldn't have done, and I could not be more proud of it.

On the day of the actual marathon, in late April, it was unusually warm. In fact, it would end up being the hottest London Marathon on record. It seemed that our idea to wear only underwear had not been so crazy after all. I was nervous – we had trained through an unusually cold winter, and I was not used to running in heat at all. But I told myself I had done this before, that this time last year I had done it in the grips of alcoholism, so how hard could today really be?

We set off and for the first nine miles, all was fine. But at ten miles, I began to fall apart. I could not bear the heat, or the chafing, or the thought that there was another sixteen or so miles to go. I felt ill. I wondered if I had sun stroke. Jada did her best to cheer me up, and we started to walk. It was very different to the year before, when I had run the whole way with a spring in my step, apart from a brief period at mile eighteen where I hit a wall – though seeing Harry and Edie in the crowd helped me get through it pretty quickly. Now it *all* felt like wall, and it made absolutely no sense to me. I was eight months sober, whereas last year I had managed only five days of sobriety before the marathon. Where were the magical, health-giving effects of my sobriety? Why was this such a fucking struggle? The fact I had only my underwear on barely registered in my mind, such was the effort just to keep moving.

It was at sixteen miles that it hit me. It was a struggle, because I wasn't running towards a pint of beer. Last year, that had been the thing that had kept me going. I had not run that marathon for the medal, but for the bender I could go on afterwards. Signing up for that race had been a way to cut down and justify my drinking, but it hadn't worked, and instead it had become almost the very point of the marathon training, more so than the running itself. If I ran for miles and miles, then I could drink. I could finally find balance, even if that balance involved running exhausting distances so that I could imbibe eight pints without feeling bad about it. Alcohol had been such a powerful force in my life, that it had actually *enabled* me to run a marathon.

Now, the only thing keeping me going was Jada. I didn't care about the medal. I had nothing to look forward to other than a lie down. It struck me then how powerful a force alcohol had exerted over my life – it was powerful enough to make me run 26.2 miles. Now that power was gone, and it all felt horrible, it all felt exactly like 26.2 miles should feel – exhausting. I limped over the finish line, and I could barely speak. I started to shiver violently. I could not believe that this time last year I had gone straight home and drunk something close to three bottles of champagne. How had I not died? It was an absolute mystery to me.

Now I felt sick. I barely had the energy to walk to a taxi. I got home, somehow climbed the stairs, and then I got into bed where I stayed for the next sixteen hours. Without the alcohol there to numb me, every bit of my body ached and screamed. It was horrifying. What had I been doing to myself all these years?

But there was no stopping me.

Not least because I couldn't have stopped, even if I had wanted to.

Rehab had been the stop, the three months I had taken out of life to deal with everything. And now I was making up for lost time.

The book I had written in record time had been turned around by my publishers in record time and was slated to come out a few weeks after the marathon (which was just about the only thing I had failed to do in record time). I was nine months into my sobriety and so far I had: judged a major book prize; travelled halfway round the world; run a marathon in my underwear and written a book. Now I was going on a tour to promote said book. Peter, who I was still seeing on a weekly basis, suggested that I seemed a little overwhelmed. I batted his suggestion away. Busy was good. Busy was a sign that the alcoholism hadn't beaten me. Busy was proof that I was thriving in my sobriety, and that life could go on as normal, or at the very least, something approaching normal. I had forgotten, of course, that my life had also been busy before my rock bottom, and that busyness hadn't done me much good *then*. But this was different, I thought, because I wasn't mixing the busy with the booze. Without a hangover, I was finding that you could be as busy as you liked.

But busy hid another truth, and that was that despite all the underwear running and the proclamations of body positivity, I was still not used to treating my body with the respect that it so deserved. I could not soothe it without also somehow destroying it. I found myself suddenly addicted to the most powerful drug on earth, the one we all first use as children: food. I would head back to my home or my hotel and I would order vast amounts of food, the fattier the better. One burger was never enough, it had to be three. I would bite in and all my stress would go. Halfway through it was as if it had never been there in the first place. By the end of the third it had reappeared, in the heartburn I felt and the sick sensation in my stomach, but I couldn't stop. I needed to fill myself with *something*. Anything. Burgers, chips, ice cream, those smoked Polish sausages they sold at the shop round the corner from my house. I would buy them in bulk and eat them one after another on the sofa, preferably while watching something completely brain-zapping like *Keeping up with the Kardashians* or *The Real Housewives of Beverly Hills*.

I tried to seduce my husband every evening, and while he liked it at first, pretty soon my demands had begun to exhaust him, and so then I started watching ridiculous amounts of porn and masturbating with the same fury I had as an adolescent. Twice, sometimes three times a day. Anything to divert myself from that feeling of failure that had been so familiar in my drinking days, and had now started to creep in again. Sometimes, to get my kicks, I would flirt with the men I queued behind in the coffee shop I was going to several thousand times a day to get my caffeine fix. It didn't matter how old they were, or what they looked like. I would fix them with a smile and start batting my eyelashes and, for the time it took the barista to make me a flat white, I would get off on misbehaving.

I had started to shop a lot. I felt I deserved it. I bought things I didn't need, things I couldn't afford. I told myself that it was OK, reminded myself that I was saving money by no longer drinking. I liked online shopping the best. I could lie in bed, on my phone, looking for things to get, to consume, to fill the same space that I had been putting the food in. Often, it didn't matter what it was. It could be a wifi extender, or a set of coat hangers, or a new case for my shattered mobile phone. I felt a little rush as I went onto my Amazon app and started to find the thing I had decided I absolutely had to have that moment – or, more realistically due to delivery times, the next day. I would announce these purchases to Harry in a tone that suggested they were a very good idea. 'I thought we could do with a heated clothes rack!' I would trill, or 'I got a Dustbuster because I know how much you hate getting the Hoover out for every tiny spill!'

At one point, I realised I had bought some guinea pigs.

Edie had been going on about how much she wanted a pet, and I had decided, one Friday after school, to take her to the big pet shop nearby to just *look* at the animals they had. Just look. Maybe a little stroke, at most. Before I knew it, we were taking delivery of two baby guinea pigs, one ginger, one black and white, both boys, but whom Edie insisted on calling Katie and Charlotte. We had travelled to the shop on the bus but such was the weight of stuff they required, we had to order a taxi as large as a van to get us home. There was the hutch. There was the hay. There were the water bottles, the wood shavings, the pellets, the food bowls. We arrived home and Edie asked what I thought Daddy would say. It hadn't occurred to me to check with him before buying the pets – we had seen them and Edie wanted them and so, because I had been such a terrible mother, we had to have them. 'I'm sure he'll be charmed with them,' I smiled. 'Absolutely charmed!'

He wasn't.

I didn't blame him. I was a woman who could barely look after herself and her daughter, let alone two gender-neutral guinea pigs who required daily clean-outs and endless attention.

But no matter what I bought, I just wanted more. More, more, more, it was the story of my life. As a child I would watch my favourite cartoon over and over again. I would listen to my favourite songs on repeat until I became sick of them. I liked things so much and so passionately that it was almost as if I had to ruin them for myself, to rid myself of the overwhelming feelings I had for them. Nothing was ever enough. The first time I drank, the cider hadn't been enough, so I had moved onto the vodka. Eventually, the booze wasn't enough, so I moved onto the cocaine. That hadn't been enough either, so I had started to have sex with anyone who would have me. But that wasn't enough, so I had looked to be saved by the love of a good man, and a baby. That hadn't been enough either, so I had gone back to the booze and the drugs. Eventually, they had stopped working too, and now, though I wasn't drinking or drugging, I was applying the same more, more, more mentality to food and shopping and wanking.

But I hadn't picked up a drink, crucially. And because I hadn't picked up a drink, I thought I was doing well. And because my diary was busy and my life was full and I *still* hadn't picked up a drink, I thought I was doing really well. I was going to meetings. I was running. I was turning up to the things I had been told to turn up to. I was good. I was really good.

It never ceases to amaze me how many layers of denial we can hide our truth under. How we can present to the world and ourselves a version of our lives that is shiny and wonderful and Instagrammable, a version we really believe to be true, despite it being nothing of the sort. How we can shout a palatable version of our story so loudly that we are completely unable to hear the true story beneath. It's mind-blowing, I have realised, how you can genuinely mean one thing, and yet three months later look back and see that you actually felt the complete opposite. How you can genuinely feel OK. How you can genuinely know you are OK. But how none of this necessarily means that you are *actually* OK.

10

The hole in my soul

B ut our subconscious knows the score.

The dreams – the drinking dreams – had been coming since the beginning, but now they stepped up with a ferocity that caused me to wake in a state of adrenalised panic. These dreams were not like the night-time vagaries that lost all their power with consciousness. These were dreams so vivid, so fleshed out and real, that they could stay with you past breakfast and hang around right until tea time.

Each dream was more or less the same. I was out with nameless, faceless friends, at a restaurant or a pub or some other establishment that served alcohol. Sometimes it would be on the river, others on a cobbled mews in a pretty area of London. All of the places were beautiful. They were scenes right out of my fantasy drinking days, the ones that involved sunlight and rosé and warmth on my skin.

My nameless, faceless friends would offer me something to drink, and I would decline their offer and tell them I was going to stick to the water. Then I would slip off under the cover of needing the toilet, and I would go to the bar and I would order a pint of lager. Just the one. I would secretly drink it, and decide that nobody need know. I could have a few drinks on the sly and then carry on pretending I was teetotal. I would not have to reset the sobriety clock, and I could continue as normal.

But then, as I drank the lager in secret, hidden from everyone, it occurred to me that my whole sobriety was a lie. I had never stopped drinking. I had spent every supposedly sober month secretly having the odd drink, and all the days I believed I had earned were a big fat falsehood. I was not sober. I was not safe. I was still in the thrall of alcohol. And I had lied to everyone: to Harry, to Edie, to Peter, to Holly, to my family, to my work, to every single person I had ever met in a twelve-step meeting. I was a fake, a fraud, a total disappointment, and I deserved to be discarded to some slag heap, never to be trusted again, losing my family and friends and job, and living out the rest of my days in the purgatory of my own making.

It was usually at this point that I would wake up, a cold sweat covering my body and a sense of relief that it had all been a dream.

But even though these dreams were only nightmares, they taunted me every waking moment of the day. They frightened me. They reminded me that I was not ever really safe from the filth that lived inside me, that it wouldn't take much to stir it up and bring it back to the surface.

When the book tour was over and things had started to die down, I started to cry. I started to cry, and I wondered if I would ever stop. I was, by now, ten months sober, inching closer and closer to that magic year that seemed like winning Olympic gold, and yet I felt utterly bereft. These were not like the tears I had cried so often in my drinking days, the tears that had been full of shame and despair. These were tears of pure sadness, tears that had been building inside me for decades and decades that I had dammed with my drinking and my drugging and in recent months my obsessive working, and now the dam had broken and they were all flooding out.

Peter told me I couldn't avoid them. He told me they would always come. He told me that I had tried my hardest, with the marathon and the book and all the other stuff, but that eventually the tears were going to catch up with me. And now they had. Now they had me good and proper.

Every time I left the house and someone innocently asked me how I was, I had to fight back the water in my eyes. I had to gulp back the force that built in my throat. Sometimes this worked and I could pretend I was fine, but other times it was a dismal failure and a breakfast meeting or a coffee would end in me breaking down over my croissant. People were largely sweet and understanding. They would put their arms around me and tell me everything was going to be OK, and their kindness was a whole other source of tears for me to sob.

I cried for my parents, for all I had put them through. I cried for my siblings for having to live in the shadow of my chaos. I cried for every boss who had had to manage me, every friend I had let down or cancelled on or not shown up for. I cried for Harry, and the incredible act of love he had committed by sticking with me. I cried for Edie, and all the times I had passed out drunk, unable to hear her cries. I cried for the baby I had ignored, for the broccoli, for all the myriad ways I had failed her. And I cried for me. I cried for me and all the things I had put my body and my brain through in the name of alcoholism.

I cried for the twelve-year-old who thought she was dying of AIDS, the one who thought she was a serial-killing paedophile. I cried for that girl who didn't get the help she so badly needed. I cried for the eighteen-year-old whose hair fell out from stress, the one who let boys do things to her she didn't neces- sarily like or want because she didn't have the self-esteem or confidence to say no. I cried for the twentysomething who hated herself so much that she regularly took cocaine, vomited up her food, and fell in love with married men who had nothing to give her and only took. I cried for the girl who really believed that pregnancy would set her right, that it would sort her out, and I cried for the girl, the woman, who had lived so much of her life in blackout. I cried and I cried, but it did not feel like self-pity. It felt like a weird kind of shedding, a necessary process I had to go through before I could move onto the next part of my life.

Holly would drive round and take me to meetings. In the car I would sob and ask her if she ever felt like this. She told me she was feeling like this while I was off running marathons and writing books. Didn't I remember? I did, now she mentioned it, and back then I had hugged her and held her hand and told her that it was all going to be OK, while wondering vaguely how I had managed to avoid crying all those tears.

Well, I hadn't. Those feelings that Peter had told me about were here, and each one felt like a tornado. I had never felt this sad before, because I had never allowed myself to feel this sad before. I had always drunk or drugged it or run it or worked it away, and now I had slowed down the sadness was on me, overwhelming and all-encompassing.

I imagined that a rug had been pulled out from beneath me. A literal, actual rug, that had been quite comfortable to stand on, and very pleasing to look at. And now it had gone, I could see all the stains it had been covering, all the bits of dirt and detritus. I wanted to scream, 'Put the rug back! Put it back this instant!' But it was too late. I had seen the muck and I could not unsee it, and so instead I was going to have to work at getting rid of it, at cleansing it from the ground beneath my feet.

Some days, most days even, I could not leave the house. I could barely dig myself out of bed. There didn't seem to be any point. The simplest tasks took an effort that I could not summon: showering, brushing my teeth, making myself breakfast. I would get Edie to school, and then I would go back to bed, pulling the curtains shut on the summer's day outside. I wondered how other people did life. I wondered if there were people out there who genuinely got about their day without any fuss, for whom minutes did not feel like hours and hours did not feel like days. I was depressed, there was no doubt about it. After all the tears I had been left curiously detached from myself, lethargic and unable to move. Then, very suddenly, as if out of nowhere, I would be overcome with complete and utter sadness. I would sink to my knees and bury my head in my hands and weep. I thought I was going to die from the sadness. Could that happen? Had that happened? The panic of this thought was awful. I could not breathe. I felt little tiny electric shocks in my chest and was convinced I was having a heart attack, the first time this had happened since I had got sober. I was having a panic attack, of course, but that knowledge didn't seem to make anything better.

My brain behaved like a depressed brain, flagellating me for being the way I was. It told me I was being lazy and silly and that I should just get up and rejoin the world, like everybody else. But I had done enough work on my mental health to know that this was a lie, that outside my darkened room there were probably other people feeling this way – or not feeling this way, as a more accurate description of depression might be.

I lay in bed. I answered the door to Holly, and went with her to meetings, where I cried again. I came back, and returned to bed. I got up and picked up Edie from school. I did the best I could under the circumstances I had found myself in, and I thought that if I got through this without picking up a drink, this awful mixture of sadness and depression and panic, then Marvel should invite me to be a member of the Avengers.

'What would your super power be?' Harry asked.

'Sitting with my feelings,' I snapped back. 'Take that, IronMan! Take that, Thor!'

I realise that there is an ocean of darkness inside me. An endless, undulating ocean of it. There is a pain in my core so tremendous, so magnificently powerful that it renders me useless; it crosses my eyes and it scalpels my soul and it flattens my body. And it has always been there. Always, always. The old me would have done anything to soothe it. Including, but not limited to, almost drinking and drugging myself to death.

But once I accept the pain, something happens to it. It becomes a clear pain, a bearable pain, a pain that I can somehow breathe and rest through until it slowly recedes. I even begin to see pain as a good thing: I wake up in the morning and I feel euphoric about the fact I am in pain and *not running away from it*. I am being with it, exploring it, trying to find the light that this darkness has to show me. Eventually, as beautiful Holly takes me to many meetings and back, it starts to occur to me that this depression is actually quite a good thing. That it's an opportunity, in a way.

I explain this to Peter. 'I think that I'm getting to some dark shit I haven't been able to get to because of my drinking. In the past, every time I felt a depression like this coming on, I would have tried to booze it away. But then I would black out, and into the blackout my brain would place all these terrible scenarios that might have happened, and so I was just stuck in this permanent attack of OCD. Now I've stopped drinking, I'm not creating those opportunities for my OCD to thrive any more, so I'm actually getting to the stuff that has been there all along, the stuff that has always been the basic problem but that I've never had a hope in hell of dealing with. Now I feel sad and depressed and all sorts of other awful things, but I think they are things I am *supposed* to be feeling. It would be weirder, in a way, if I didn't, if I'd just gone to rehab and that had been that in twelve weeks. I mean, when I think about it, when I *really* think about it, a lot of stuff has happened in the last few years. A lot of it has been great, some of it not so great, but I have not allowed myself time to process any of it. I've just been rushing around like a lunatic, trying to work out what the next thing is. So of course, now, with a bit of time to reflect on what's happened, I'm going to collapse. I'm doing what I should have done months ago. I'm basically falling apart! But that's OK! That's good! Because

255

sometimes, you need to fall apart in order to be able to put yourself back together again!'

Peter smiles at me. I smile back. 'I never thought I'd say these words, but I'm so glad I'm feeling this sadness. So, so glad. I can't wait to see what is on the other side.' I begin to cry again. It would still be some time before I got to the other side, but we were at least making progress. We at least knew it was there.

Was this all that sanity was, in the end? The knowledge that you were not OK, and that that was OK. You didn't have to be fine the whole time. The world didn't owe anyone 'fine' the whole time. You didn't have to always be happy. You just had to live.

That first summer of sobriety, it felt like the world was on fire. It felt as if I had entered a wormhole to another dimension. There was a never-ending heatwave that made London feel more like Athens. England had got to the semi-final of the World Cup, and it seemed as if the whole country was outside drinking. When I could leave the house, I felt like I was wading through treacle. It was the same temperature inside my body as outside it. I drew the curtains now out of necessity: all the shops had long ago sold out of air-conditioning units and fans. Sometimes I would walk to Sainsbury's, and spend hours pacing the frozen food aisles in a sort of catatonic state. It was often the only place I felt truly safe, not to mention cool.

In the winter, you could somehow ignore alcohol. You could march past the pubs without looking inside; you were not faced with it everywhere you went, like a malevolent ex-boyfriend who was stalking you. Now it was all over the place. It was in the park, as people had picnics, it was on the street, as people stood outside bars and pubs holding ice-cold pints of lager, and it was flashed on every TV screen as some news reporter narrated a segment about fans watching the World Cup. I felt as if this heatwave was a test from the universe: pass this and you could handle anything sober.

I thought about alcohol a lot, about some magic way of recapturing the buzz that you got sitting in a beer garden at the beginning of a good session. With all the brain power in my possession, I could not. I sat in the dark at home, scrolling through Instagram, looking at pictures of people holding great big glasses of some bright orange drink called Aperol Spritz. I had somehow missed this boat, and realised I would probably die without ever knowing what one tasted like. Or at least I *hoped* I would. I felt like I was clinging onto my sobriety with one weakened finger.

One night, I knew that Harry was out for work. I resented him for this, imagining drinks at some bar overlooking the river, and I spent the whole day fantasising about what it would be like. I made a plan. I would go to the Co-Op and I would buy some of those non-alcoholic beers I had been warned off. The need for some sort of garden sitting with a cold drink drowned out the words of Peter: non-alcoholic drinks are for non-alcoholics. I marched down to the supermarket, and set about buying some for myself to enjoy later that evening.

I stood in front of the non-alcoholic and low-alcohol section, that I had no idea existed. I knew I had to be careful. The drink I chose had to be 0 per cent alcohol, not 0.9 per cent, as some non-alcoholic beers were. As small as that amount might seem to most people, it was actually quite a lot for someone who hadn't drunk alcohol for a while, and I had heard tales in recovery of people relapsing on them, of having a few low-alcohol drinks before moving onto something harder.

I stared at all the drinks on display, amazed at this thriving part of the drinks industry. If you could drink alcohol, why wouldn't you drink alcohol? Who were all the nutters out there actively choosing to partake in a non-alcoholic beer of an evening, when you could have a pint of the real stuff instead? I supposed they were nutters like me, who had had their drinking privileges taken away from them. A couple stood three metres away from me, loading a trolley up with sparkling wine and bottles of actual beer. They laughed and smiled together as if this was the most normal thing in the world, and I hated them for their easy, carefree existence.

I opted for a four-pack of a zero-alcohol beer. Then I thought I should get two four-packs of zero-alcohol beer, just in case. I didn't know what that just in case was, but I allowed the idea to sit there with me as I walked to the till and plonked my booty down on the counter. I asked the woman on duty for a packet of Marlboro Golds, and she said, 'Are you having a party?' I laughed hollowly. The idea that any of this might constitute a good time seemed absurd.

I walked home in the stifling heat and put half my zero-alcohol beers in the fridge, the other half in the freezer. I went to pick Edie up from a play date, and when we got home I gave her a quick shower, brushed her teeth, and put her to bed. She said, 'Aren't you going to read me a story?' And I replied that I couldn't tonight because it was late and she needed to get to sleep. She looked at me curiously, as if I had gone quite mad, which to be fair I probably had. It was only 6.45 p.m. Outside, the sun had blazed the plastic lids of the bins in the front garden into a warped shape, so that they would never fit properly again. I had forgotten that evening last September when I had plotted that last-night-of-drinking-that-never-was. It was almost identical to this one, in all ways but one: back then I had been planning to drink alcohol, and now I was planning to drink some fake version of it. I felt like a small child eagerly awaiting her Babycham. It was pathetic. But then I felt pathetic.

I went down to the kitchen and realised there was a slight spring in my step. I headed for the freezer, and removed the four zero-alcohol beers, placing three in the fridge and keeping the other one in my hand. It had been a long time since I had gone to get an ice-cold drink on a summer's evening.

I went to the cupboard and I got a pint glass. Then, realising the one bottle would not fill it, I went back to the fridge to fetch another one. I rustled in the cutlery drawer for a bottle opener. I felt naughty, like I was doing something really bad, and I am ashamed to say I got a buzz from that feeling. I opened the bottles, and watched as the lids fell pleasingly onto the counter. I felt their serrated edges on my fingers, the smoothness of the plastic in the cap. I took them to the bin and threw them in the recycling. It felt good. Then I returned to my bottles which I took great care to empty into my pint glass without creating a froth. Did zero-alcohol beer even make a froth? No, it seemed it did not.

I held the glass in my hands, and felt its pleasing weight, its lovely low temperature. I put it to my forehead and gasped at the cold. I looked straight through it, at the amber liquid, and the bubbles inside it. This felt so normal. It felt so right.

I went to the garden with my pint of zero-alcohol lager and my packet of fags and I sat down at the table at which I had spent so many evenings, drinking and smoking and gassing and blacking out. I took a sip of my fake lager and lit a fag and for a moment I felt release. I felt relief. It tasted like the real deal. But a few sips in and I realised it did not *feel* like the real deal, so I gulped that one down and went to top myself up. I did this again and again and again, chain-smoking as I went, until suddenly I realised that an hour and a half had passed and most of the cigarettes were gone and I had finished all eight bottles of zero-alcohol beer.

I sat down on the kitchen floor and I wept.

It was as if alcohol had never left me, like rehab had never happened, like my love for booze had never, ever gone away. Maybe it hadn't. Maybe it never would. Maybe, like some toxic, abusive relationship, I would still occasionally long for it, for the cold cloak of oblivion it could somehow provide.

But I knew, in that moment, that I did not want to go back to it. The next logical stage from my non-alcoholic beer binge was an actual alcoholic beer binge, and for the sake of my daughter and her wellbeing, I could not let that happen again. What would be the point? Really, what possible use could it serve? I had made drinking so unappealing to myself that there would be no nice way to do it – I would have to do it in secret, by myself, in dark corners of hostile pubs, lying to everyone I loved including myself. It would not be fun. I would never again be able to recapture the moments of euphoria I thought I had in my early days of drinking, because now I knew them all to be a terrible charade, a magic effect created by smoke and mirrors and deception. If I drank alcohol now, I would only be putting off the misery I felt until I stopped drinking, when the misery would come back with interest. It was like borrowing wellbeing from my future, and I had realised I didn't like being in debt to anyone, least of all myself.

Alcohol is a depressant masquerading remarkably well as a relaxant, an Oscar-winning actor that had had me fooled for years. But it fooled me no longer. The treat was actually the trick, and I was not going to fall for it any more. I was just going to have to get through this. Being frustrated and sad and angry was not going to kill me, but alcohol might.

And anyway, I was starting to realise that alcohol was not really my problem. It was just a symptom of it. My problem was that I could not deal with life, and that was OK, that was just fine, just so long as I kept to the programme I had learnt in rehab and the twelve-step meetings in my pocket and stuck to it.

I had learnt that the desire to be happy all the time had made me profoundly unhappy. There was a hole in my soul, but there was a hole in *everyone's* soul. There wasn't a human alive who didn't feel anxiety or despair or sadness. The key to contentment, I supposed – and contentment felt like a better place to be aiming for than happiness, given that I felt you could be content with any state of mind just as long as you accepted it as all part of the human condition – was how you chose to treat the hole, and how you chose to treat the hole depended on a complex variety of factors that were biological, environmental and circumstantial. Some people chose to accept the hole in their soul, and do their best to live a life that did not make it any bigger. But other people tried to close the hole, by stuffing things inside it: alcohol, drugs, sex, gambling, food, shopping. The only problem with the stuffing method was that it actually made the hole in the soul bigger. It was like spraying emotional CFCs on the hole in the ozone layer. The only way to deal with the void was simply to acknowledge its presence and to treat yourself with kindness when you felt yourself staring into the depths of it. To find healthy ways of living with it. I realised that, in the months since I had left rehab, I had been trying to stuff all sorts of things other than alcohol and drugs into the hole: food, random purchases on Amazon, masturbation. I was still trying to change the way I felt: I was just doing it with burgers instead of booze. I wondered: would there ever be a time when I could enjoy something without obsessively overdoing it and ruining it for myself? When I could find peace?

Life rumbled on, a sweltering sweat bucket of a summer that at times I thought would never end. But at other times, I realised, I didn't *want* it to end. Harry, Edie and I went to Somerset for a few days to stay in a shed that had been billed as a glamping unit, and we howled and howled with laughter as we roasted marshmallows on the fire outside. We booked a barn in France for two weeks towards the end of August, and were amused to find that we seemed to have arrived in the only part of Europe not experiencing a heatwave. For the first few days, we stayed inside, watching the rain sweep over the swimming pool. We played games. We drew. We lit fires. We ate. We didn't drink. Eventually the sun came out and we spent our days teaching Edie to dive, and playing with water guns. I read many novels. I read a 700-page one about trees, and an 800-page one about Nigeria. This in itself was a progress unimaginable a year ago.

I thought back to the summer before, the one when I had done my very best to kill myself. I realised that, for almost 365 days, I had woken up every morning and not immediately wanted to die. The thought had still sometimes occurred to me, but usually not until much later in the day, and even then I was almost always able to dismiss it out of hand as something ludicrous that was not worth taking in the slightest bit seriously. For almost 365 days, I had made the decision to look after myself. For almost 365 days, I had committed to my family rather than my alcoholism. For almost 365 days, I had lived consciously. Sometimes painfully – often painfully, in fact – but never in blackout. For 365 days, I had faced down the truth and my fears and nothing truly terrible had happened, nothing new that was terrible, anyway.

And every day I had chosen to live this way, I had been stoking the fire of self-esteem within myself. Sometimes the stoking action was so tiny as to be almost imperceptible. But it was there and it was happening and it all added up to something that was hard to describe in words, at least to someone who hadn't gone out of their way to destroy themselves. I had instead been *healing* myself, and it was a tribute to how much healing I had done that the word didn't make me cringe. I was not the toxic woman who had rocked up at rehab and refused to hear that she was an addict. I was not the cynical woman who would spend time with people she didn't know or like just so she could feed the addiction she denied she had. I was not the human who had been so hollowed out by self-loathing that she would rather hang out with virtual strangers taking drugs than with her own husband and daughter.

What had happened in the last year was real magic, not the alcohol that performed its tricks with almost immediate effect: this was so slow that it had gone about its work without ever really being detected. I had been made comfortable. I was experiencing something that maybe, just maybe felt like contentment.

On the morning of 27 August 2018, I woke up in the barn in France and realised I was one.

I had done a whole turn of the sun without picking up an alcoholic drink.

It was a miracle. It was an absolute fucking miracle.

And what was more of an absolute fucking miracle was the fact that I didn't expect anything of this day. At the beginning of this journey, I had imagined fireworks and balloons on your first sobriety birthday. I had imagined a big party, full of fruit mocktails and people telling me how amazing I was. I had imagined that I would be some spiritual guru who lit up a room purely through the power of the positive vibes I gave off.

But instead, I rolled over, said good morning to my husband, and smiled. Then I went to the kitchen and made myself some coffee, went outside onto the verandah, and sat in my pyjamas watching the sun come up, smoking fags and drinking my caffeine.

I texted Holly congratulations. She immediately texted them right back. We made plans to speak that night. I went back into the house and looked in on Edie. She was sleeping soundly, as was Harry. I tiptoed quietly to the cupboard and got my gym kit out. I put it on and crept back to the kitchen where I found my trainers. I laced them up and I left the house and I ran. I ran and I ran and I ran, five miles of sweat and tears and joy.

When I returned, Edie was standing in the garden jumping up and down. She had a balloon in her hand. 'Happy birthday, Mummy! Happy birthday!' she said, and in her excitement as she hugged me, she let the balloon go. I held her in my arms and we watched it float up into the sky. Then we went into the kitchen where Harry greeted me with another cup of coffee and a breakfast spread of dreams.

'Pretty proud of you right now,' he said, pulling me into a bear hug.

At the breakfast table, Edie asked why it was I got two birthdays. One day I would explain to her properly, but for now I said I was like the Queen. This seemed to please her, and it worked for me. Later that day, we caught our flight home. We got the train back from the airport, and rolled our suitcases through the last heat of the summer to our house. It was lovely and cool inside. We unpacked, put the washing on, had some dinner and went to bed. I had forgotten to call Holly, so sent her a message explaining how exhausted I was and asked if it would be possible to speak tomorrow. She replied immediately. 'Don't you worry. We have the rest of our lives to talk xx'

Epilogue: All is well, my darling

They say that for the first five years of recovery, you are basically a baby. Like most of the clichés I hear in sobriety, it is true. Like a baby, or a small child, I must be fed and watered regularly, and get a good night's sleep. I need to do what I am told, and accept that this programme I have put myself in the care of knows better than I do. The longer I go without a drink, the less I realise I know. But that isn't a bad thing. It's a wonderful thing, this knowledge that life will always be full of new things to learn.

Every day has the power to surprise me, to teach me new things. Quitting alcohol has not been the miracle cure for the lows I have experienced since childhood, no more than taking it up had been. But it

269

has taught me a way to deal with them. My OCD, such a huge and negative part of my life, has now dwindled to almost nothing. It is still there, but I now have the strength to right-size it, to be bigger than it. If you had told this to me ten years ago, I would not have been able to believe it.

I still get depressed. I still have days when I cannot dig myself out of bed. Terrible things have happened in my sobriety. My godson's mother developed an auto-immune illness that destroyed her liver. I sat with her in her hospital ward as she awaited her transplant, brushing her hair and helping her to rub cream on her beautiful face, and we joked darkly about the unfairness of a world where she, a woman who barely drank, needed a liver transplant, while her alcoholic friends like myself found themselves in peak health. We made plans for her recovery. I would be her sober buddy – not that she really needed one, given she had never drunk that much in the first place. But I never saw her again. She died a few weeks later, before her youngest son turned one. My godson was just four. I felt the fog of grief, but not as profoundly as her immediate family. I was relieved that sobriety made it possible for me to do the job she had given me: to be godmother to her son. I did not want to dwell on how useless I would have been to my friend and her firstborn had I still been drinking.

Another friend was diagnosed with cancer. She asked

me to come along to her diagnosis, to take notes. I knew that I would not have been extended that honour if I had not been sober.

Nothing special or meaningful in my life exists without my sobriety.

Harry and I are still together. We still argue. Sometimes, he goes out and gets steamingly drunk with his mates, and when he comes home slurring his words I am relieved that this is no longer my world.

I still see Peter once a week, like clockwork.

The guinea pigs are thriving. I just built an outdoor hutch and run for them, so they have plenty of space to play in.

Yes, I really did write the above sentence.

At the time of going to press, Holly and I are two years, 6 months and 13 days sober. But it's never a done thing. I would like to be able to promise to you that I will stay sober forever and ever and ever, but if I have learnt anything in this process, it is that it is not in my gift to be able to predict the ending of my story. I have no idea what will happen to me tomorrow, or the day after that. But if I could give you a happy ending, then it would be this:

It is late September, two years after I found myself in rehab. I am on my local common with Edie, who has just gone back to school. Year two! Today she can read and write and know that she will be put to bed by a woman who will always, always read her a story, even when she doesn't want one. I have picked her up from school with two pink buckets in my hand, buckets from a holiday to Dorset earlier in the year, when we stayed with my doctor friend and her kids in a rented cottage for a week, and we swam in the sea and ate delicious food and dug sandcastles and joined the National Trust because it made sense given how often we went to their properties and had to pay for parking.

I have the buckets with me because it is the time of year when conkers fall from the horse chestnut tree, and on our local common there is a particular bounty at the moment. I have promised Edie we will spend the afternoon collecting as many conkers as possible. I have promised her that we will stuff our pockets full of them, and then we will take them home and count them out and play with them in the garden.

We get up to the common and we have some competition from other kids, but we are confident that we will still manage a handsome harvest. We start to pick them up, carefully avoiding the spiky cases they have fallen from. I focus on one particular conker. It is beautiful and big and in ruddy good health. I feel its smooth body, and feel calm and collected and *contained*. I look up at Edie, who is attempting to balance as many conkers as possible in her bucket, with limited success. Her bucket is so stuffed with the things that

272

they keep rolling out and away from her. She laughs as she runs after them. I tell her I think that maybe we have enough.

We start to walk home, through vibrant red leaves. I have one of her hands in mine, while my other holds my bucket of conkers. We arrive at our house and I put my bucket down and look for my keys. I unlock the door and we go inside, taking off our shoes and coats and heading into the living room. We start to lay out our conkers on the floor. I hold one in my hand, turning it softly like the world's loveliest stress ball. The world is still turning. The conkers are still falling. I look at Edie and I think: all is well, my darling.

Resources

For honest information about drugs, and help and advice in the UK: www.talktofrank.com; 0300 1236600

For a list of NHS and private services: www.adfam.org.uk

Action on Addiction are a UK charity providing support to people who need rehab, as well as a wealth of resources for those battling addiction issues: www.actiononaddiction.org.uk

Alcoholics Anonymous: alcoholics-anonymous.org.uk; 0800 9177 650

Glorious Rock Bottom

Narcotics Anonymous: ukna.org; 0300 999 1212

Al Anon – is for families of people with addiction issues:
al-anonuk.org.uk; 0800 0086 811

Acknowledgements

There are so many people I need to thank, not just for supporting me through the writing of this book, but also for supporting me through my active alcoholism and the process of getting sober. Every person in recovery has at least 100 people behind them who have helped them get to where they are, so I apologise if I forget anyone.

To my agent Janelle Andrew, and my editor Sarah Emsley: thank you for never moving from my side as this process unfurled. Thank you also to everyone at Headline and PFD who have supported me.

To the people who have held my hand and laughed with me when times got tough: Laura Wilkins, Emma Campbell, Martha Freud, Olivia Bridges, Louise

Wilkinson, Nikki Minors, Rosie Thomas, Helena Marchese, Jane Cullen, Meredith Davies, Rebecca Priestley, Daisy Lewis, Vicky Harper, Jane Bruton, Ellie Steafel, Laura Dimmock Jones. I am lucky to have the world's best girl gang in my life.

To everyone I was in treatment with, and every single person I have met in the twelve-step meetings: thank you.

To Holly: what would I have done without you?

To my mum, dad, sister, brother, cousins, aunts, uncles, in-laws: thank you for never wavering, even though I gave you plenty of opportunities to.

Finally, to Harry and Edie: we got this.